Montana's Child

A Memoir of Life in Big Sky Country

Gwen Ellis

Seaside Creative Publishers

Montana's Child
© 2015 by Gwen Ellis
All rights reserved.

No part of this publication may be reproduced, stored in a retrieval system, or transmitted in any form or by any means—electronic, mechanical, photocopy, recording, scanning, or otherwise—without the prior written permission of the copyright holder, except as provided by USA copyright law.

All Scriptures are taken from the Holy Bible, New International Version, copyright © 1973, 1978, 1984 by the International Bible Society. Used by permission of Zondervan Publishing House. The "NIV" and "New International Version" trademarks are registered in the United States Patent and Trademark Office by International Bible Society.

Cover design: Troy Russell
Cover photo: Gwen Ellis
Editing and interior design: Seaside Creative Services, Inc.
ISBN 978-0-99645692-0

To Grace and Orbrie Ellis, my parents,
who taught us how to live and ultimately how to die.

To my beloved brothers Ray Ellis and Glen Ellis,
who shared these experiences with me.

To my children Wendy Weising and Mark Weising,
to whom I tried to impart the values I learned
as a child growing up in Montana,
and who continue to make my life worth living.

Montana's Child

Contents

Introduction 9

1. Getting Born in Montana 11
2. Oh, Brother—Brothers!................................15
3. A Light in a Dark Place 21
4. Puppies Under the House 27
5. A New Home 33
6. Christmas Came Early 39
7. Trains 49
8. The Great Remodel......................................57
9. Getting into Hot Water 63
10. The Big Yellow Cat.......................................67
11. Camping Extraordinaire 69
12. Making Stew on a Grander Scale.................77
13. The Williamsburg of the West......................81
14. Let's Go to the Dump!..................................87
15. Bees and a Big White Goose.......................91
16. Potato Picking..95
17. One Hundred Years and Counting 101
18. Working in Montana 105
19. The Garden 111
20. Skippy...123
21. Watermelons in the Snow 129

22. Fish Stories	135
23. A Skinny Black Cat	139
24. The Big Blackfoot River	143
25. Riot!	151
26. Giants and Gemstones	157
27. Rodeos and All Things Western	163
28. Swimming Holes	167
29. A Forever Kind of Love	171
Epilogue: All Things Come to an End	177
Fifty Bests About Montana	181

Introduction

Long before dozens of celebrities discovered the majesty of its shining mountains and sparkling rivers and waving fields of grain, there was Montana. And there were the farmers, stockmen, miners, and lumberjacks—rugged men—who carved the state from wilderness and made it one of the last, best places on earth.

Montana is many things to many people. To me, it is home. No matter where I go or what I do, there is an invisible thread tugging at my heart and pulling me toward the high mountain valley where I was born. Mom and Dad are gone now and I don't get "home" as often as I'd like, but I find my heart turning there often. The Deer Lodge Valley is as peaceful a place as you can find on earth. One day, when my life is over, I will lie in the quiet cemetery where my parents and grandparents are buried. There, Mount Powell, the ancient mountain whose face is as familiar to me as my own, will watch over all of us until Gabriel's trumpet sounds and we meet together in the air.

It has long been my dream to write about my Montana—to share with you the love that I have for it. I want you to breathe deeply of its air so crisp and clean you think it newly minted. I want you to step out the back door in the evening and be overwhelmed by the delicious odor of new-cut hay wafting down from the tableland when farmers start to cut and stack it for the long bitter winter ahead. I want you to hike beside me and see bear grass with its huge white plumes waving in the summer breeze beside crystal-clear streams. Perhaps in spring we'll find fields of deep pink shooting stars, or perhaps you'll even find the tiny pale pink bitterroot flower that blooms such a short time and then is gone.

You can learn all the facts and stats imaginable about the state from travel and history books. That's not what I want to share with you. I want to share what it was like in Montana during the 1940s when houses had no electric dryers or dishwashers and many people burned wood and coal to keep warm. I want you to know how essential to our diet was the wild game taken from the forests and the homegrown food from our garden. I want you to smell the scent of metal that clung to my father's clothes when he returned each day from "the smelter." I want you to see the homemade and homegrown people with fiercely independent spirits who fill the state with a powerful and creative can-do attitude that exists yet today.

Please come with me.

Gwen Ellis

1

Getting Born in Montana

I was born in 1938 at the end of the Great Depression when the country was dragging itself up out of a very dark time. In Deer Lodge, Montana, people were poor, and my parents and all the rest of the family were *very* poor. Those days were tough and left scars on the survivors—ugly scars of poverty that those who lived through the Depression carried to the end of their lives.

My parents met when Mother was fourteen and Daddy was seventeen. They dated and waited for each other to grow up before they married. Six years later, Grace finally walked to the altar to marry her tall, strong husband with the strange-sounding name—Orbrie.

In those days, people didn't worry about having a career. They considered themselves fortunate if they had a job. They found work where they could and worked hard to keep their jobs. Daddy had a succession of jobs, mostly farm work and manual labor. Shortly after he and Mother were married, he worked on a construction crew that was building a dam on Rock Creek up in the mountains west of Deer Lodge.

One day he came home in the middle of the day. Mother was surprised and asked, "What are you doing home?" He answered, "The cook got drunk and the boss fired him. The men are hungry and refuse to work unless they eat. Do you think you could cook for them?"

Mom's mouth fell open. She was a twenty-year-old bride who had been married only a few weeks. Could she do it? She didn't know.

"I could try," she reluctantly told him, "but there's just one thing I can't do."

"What's that?" he asked.

"I can't make the pancakes. You'll have to do that."

They agreed he would make the pancakes, she would do the rest of the cooking, and he would help her clean up. They packed a few clothes, climbed into their pickup truck, and headed for the cookhouse at the construction site. Although the distance from town to the lake was only fifteen miles, they didn't travel back and forth each day. They took up residence in a small drafty cabin that Dad declared "you could throw a cat through the cracks in the wall." So Mom cooked, Dad made pancakes, and the men ate and worked.

They hadn't lived at the lake very long when one night a mountain rat decided to move in with them. My mom was five-foot-four-inches tall and only weighed about 110 pounds soaking wet. She took one look at that rat and fled to the top of the table in her nightgown while her brave groom chased the rodent. Well, that threw the rat into a panic, and it decided the table would be a good place to escape the lanky mad man with the broom.

When the rat (who was probably as terrified as Mom) started up the leg of the table, she moved to the far corner. Picture it: there was Mom in her nightgown on one end of the table, and the rat was coming up a leg on the other end. I rather imagine Dad was so tickled and laughing at the ridiculousness of it all, that he was having trouble hitting the rat with the broom. Just in time, he regained his composure and delivered the fatal blow, swept the dead rat out of the cabin, and took his frightened bride in his arms.

In the fall, the construction site closed down for the bitter winter that would soon follow, and Mom and Dad moved back to town. They moved into a little house on Milwaukee Avenue. Dad was proud of his little place and his bride and his life. I was conceived just before Christmas.

The next nine months slid by. Soon it was September and time for my birth. Dad was back working on the dam. Mom, in her third trimester of pregnancy, had not volunteered to cook that year. In September, when a concerned husband went to work, he told her, "If you feel the slightest twinge, you get to your mother's house. I'll get there as soon as I can."

About noon on September 13, she felt different than she ever had before and decided maybe it would be wise to go to her mother's house. So did she ask the neighbor to take her? Did she call a cab? (What's a cab?) Did she at least phone her family? No. Neither she nor my grandparents had a phone, so she couldn't call for someone to come for her. What she did was to walk more than a mile to her mother's house. The doctor came, and I was born in my grandmother's front bedroom less than three hours later.

Dad got home in time for my birth, and I was put in his arms moments after. He had always had a wrinkly forehead, and Mom would say again and again, "Don't scrunch up your forehead like that."

"Like what?" he'd ask as he raised his eyebrows and scrunched up his forehead. Mom took one look at me with my scrunched up newborn forehead and decided it was genetic. He scrunched up his forehead till the day he died, and I will too.

When I was two weeks old, even though it was the beginning of October and getting kind of crispy in the evenings in the high mountains, Mom and Dad loaded me into a big wicker baby buggy, covered me with a blanket, and walked to church. They made the trek pushing the buggy Sunday mornings and Sunday evenings until the snow came. That became the pattern for the rest of my life: church twice on Sundays, including Sunday school, and once on Wednesdays for Bible study.

Mom and Dad had found a faith they could cling to throughout their lives. They had found a faith that worked in the good times and in the bad. They had found friendship and nurture in the church, and the church became the center of our family's social and spiritual life. It remained so throughout all my growing-up years.

2

Oh, Brother — Brothers!

Two and a half years after I was born, my brother, Glen, was born. By now Dad had gone to work at the Anaconda Company and we had moved to a tiny house in the inappropriately named miniscule town of Opportunity—next door to Anaconda, Montana, and the smelter where Daddy worked.

I remember a baby crib appearing behind the door of the room that served as living room and bedroom for all of us. The crib was brown. It now seems like an odd color for a crib, but truthfully, it was probably a hand-me-down and brown paint was cheap. I asked why the bed was there and was told that it was for my new baby brother or sister—whichever it might be. (In those days you didn't get to know ahead of time.)

When the time came for the baby to be born, we went once again to Grandma Cole's house in Deer Lodge, twenty-three miles away. My grandmother tucked me into bed on the sofa in the living room, just ten feet from where my mother lay in labor. About all I remember is that someone awakened me and told me I had a new baby brother.

It's strange the things that stick in your mind about an event like that. I remember that the sofa, like the baby bed, was brown and the fabric was chenille. I was sleeping under a yellow and white quilt, which I'm sure my grandmother had made. I don't remember any great emotional response except a sense of wonder that while I had been sleeping, a baby brother had come to be part of my life.

Eighteen months later, Ray was born into our family and our circumstances had changed. Daddy now had insurance from the smelter, so Ray was born in the local hospital operated by the Sisters of Charity. The post-World War II philosophy was that mothers were to stay in bed for two full weeks after giving birth, and they spent most of that time in the hospital. Children *never* visited the maternity ward. Glen and I were trundled off to Grandma Cole's house to be cared for during my mother's "confinement."

Mom never spent much time in labor. Her babies came easily and quickly. When Ray was born, he was born in a caul. Unborn babies are contained within a membrane in the womb, and once in a great while an infant is born with that membrane draped over its head. Being born in a caul is a somewhat rare occurrence, and legend has it that anyone so born is destined to greatness. There have been several of the truly greats of history, including Shakespeare, who were born this way.

I once asked my mother if she had planned to have another baby so soon after Glen's birth. She said, "No, but because we hadn't planned another baby so soon, the one that came was very special." I thought that was a very sweet attitude.

Ray was born two days before my fourth birthday, and for the reasons I've just mentioned—ten days in the hospital for new mothers, no children allowed—I celebrated my birthday without her. Daddy came by Grandma's house after work on my birthday and dropped off a new tricycle for me. It was a deep aqua-blue color. At that moment, I really didn't want the tricycle; I wanted my mommy. Mom and Dad seldom left us with babysitters.

Once in a while we would stay with Grandma so that Mom could go hunting with Dad, but that was about it. Women didn't work outside the home, and so, as a four year old, I had spent very little time away from my mother. Being separated from her was a hugely traumatic event for me. Daddy wasn't really available either, as he was either working or visiting my mom in the hospital. And then it got worse for me.

My grandmother had some old crony friends who were terrible gossips. I was the kind of kid who would keep real quiet so I would not be observed. Then I could listen to what was being said. Well, one day that didn't work. Mrs. Coombs (we always called her Mrs. Coombs and never by a first name, and so did everyone else, even Gramma) came to visit. The two ladies were gossiping up a storm, and I was listening when I was discovered. They went into the back bedroom and closed the door to tell their secrets. I tried to open the door and go into the bedroom too, or at least listen at the door. But I was told I had "big ears" and needed to go away.

I was crushed. When Daddy came, I raced out to the car, pulled back my long hair to expose my ears, and said, "Mrs. Coombs said I have big ears. My ears aren't big, are they, Daddy?" He laughed. I was dead serious, and he laughed. Of course, from my grownup vantage point, I understand why he laughed, but at time I was devastated. And that wasn't the end of my ordeal.

A few days later, just before my mother was released from the hospital, Gramma Cole decided to take Glen and me to Washington State to visit her daughter, Edith. My grandfather had died only about two months before Ray was born. I'm sure the stress on my grandmother at this point must have been almost overwhelming. Because Grandfather had worked on the railroad, Gramma had a life-long railroad pass and could travel anywhere in the country where a train went. I'm sure she escaped with us to a place where she could have some emotional and physical support. Caring for two children under the age of four must have been tough for her at this time.

I remember absolutely nothing about the train trip. I do remember that it was sunny and warm in the Skagit Valley of Washington. My aunt and uncle lived in a ramshackle old house. There was a pear tree in the yard, but there was no grass. The yard at the front of the house was filled with pea gravel. Glen sat on the ground with an oversized spoon, feeding that pea-gravel into the large end of an old phonograph's speaker that had long since been a useful part of an operating phonograph. The speaker formed a huge funnel and rattled in a lovely way as the gravel hit its sides.

Glen was a blue-eyed, blond, curly haired child. He sat and played in the sun all day long, and by the end of the day, his skin was fried. He looked more like a lobster than a baby. I was enraged that the grownups had let this happen to my little brother.

The toilet seat of that old house was split. I was afraid to sit on it for fear of being pinched or getting a splinter. So I stopped using the toilet and started wetting my pants. I detested the way hot urine felt running down my leg, but it was better than sitting on that seat and risking injury. I'm sure the adults thought I was regressing because of the birth of a new baby. I know I was derided with, "Only babies wet their pants."

After what to me seemed a lifetime, we boarded the train and went home. Home to Deer Lodge. Home to Mother and Daddy. Home to where we would be safe from derision and jabbed remarks. Home to where we could go to Sunday school and church and have stories read to us.

But my trauma was not over. When we arrived at our house, Mother was there, but she didn't look like the mother I remembered. That mother had been fat with a tummy sticking out in front. This mother was skin and bones. And there was someone there helping her with the washing—someone I didn't know.

Mother was glad, so glad, to see us, but I wouldn't go to her. I wasn't sure she was really my mother. She and Gramma chattered away happily, catching up on all the latest news. Slowly, so slowly, I began to relax and feel at home. Soon I slipped over to her for a reassuring hug and kiss. She was still my mother. She still loved me. And now I had another brother—a tiny, five-pound brother for whom I instantly took responsibility. I loved him immediately, and since I was now the big sister, I got to hold him.

As I've looked back to those years, I realize the stress a young child might face in similar circumstances. First, my grandfather died and I was taken to see him laid out in the funeral home. I had never experienced death before, not even the death of a pet. My mother—hugely pregnant at the time—went totally to pieces with her grief, and I was horribly frightened by her reaction. Then, days later, she was whisked off to a hospital, which had never happened before. I was separated from her, and I was not used to that. My daddy was distracted just when I needed him so much. Next, some old ladies ridiculed me, and then we were taken on a train to a new location far from home where everything was different. And finally, when I returned home, my mother didn't resemble the Mama I knew.

Looking back, I know the adults did the best they knew how to do. We were cared for and were never in any harm, but I have born the marks of the abandonment that happened then and still fight it today. While I have long since forgiven the adults in my life for the way they treated a sensitive child—a child who really didn't understand what was happening and couldn't express her needs—I have come to realize how tender a child is, that we adults don't always know what's happening in a child's mind, and how this can affect that child for life.

Getting born in Montana was good, for while life was hard, winters were brutal, and the pay for hard labor was small, it was a safe place where creativity could flourish and where love and peace reigned. It was a place of nurture not only physically but also spiritually as well.

3

A Light in a Dark Place

On December 6, 1941, life in Deer Lodge, Montana, was going along like most any other December day anyone could remember. The crisp, cold air was full of sunshine—typical for Montana—and the "big sky" sported a few puffy clouds coasting over Mount Powell from west to east. True, there was a war in far-off Europe that was worrisome, but in those days before television, the sounds of guns and bombs couldn't be heard there in the mountains. It was difficult to believe there was a war at all.

In this little town, proud parents attended basketball games played by their high school children. Folks shoveled snow from their walkways and chatted at the corner drugstore, speculating about what might happen next in Europe. In those days, before people had clothes dryers, moms hung laundry on the clothesline in their backyards and in a few hours retrieved them. With reddened hands, they wrestled freeze-dried sheets and board-stiff blue chambray work shirts into laundry baskets.

At night when the air was crystal clear and very cold, these same people tuned in their radios to learn the news outside their peaceful valley. And on this quiet Saturday night, mothers laid out clothing for services that would be held the next morning in one of the half-dozen churches in town. Finally, all over town, lights went out and everyone slept an unknowing sleep.

The next day, Japanese warplanes swooped down on Pearl Harbor and dropped payload after payload of bombs on the American fleet at anchor there. When the folks of Deer Lodge turned on their radios, they learned the unthinkable had happened. America had been attacked. America had been bombed, and there were thousands of casualties. Soon President Roosevelt would address the nation, telling not only what had happened but also perhaps giving some clue as to the course of action the government would take.

On December 6, the world seemed like a fairly safe place in spite of the conflict in Europe. On December 7, everything changed forever. Fear became a constant companion—the fear and anxiety of not knowing what would come next.

I was very young when America was attacked and do not remember the event, but I do remember a few years later when the war had dragged on and on. I remember my uncles looking so splendid in their uniforms when they came home on furlough. I remember shortages and rationing and food stamps. I remember sirens and air wardens and blackouts. I remember grownups' serious war talk around the table on Sunday after church when family or friends came to dinner. I remember Dad leaning on the back fence and discussing the latest current events with neighbors. And I remember in first grade when one of our classmates was absent because his father had been killed in the war. I thought that was the most horrible thing I had ever known.

I remember it all and so much more, but what I remember most about those days was fear—my fear. Even though I was very young, I felt the black unformed cloud of anxiety that hung over the entire land. I felt that same fear on September 11, 2001, as I saw with my own eyes a plane fly into the second World Trade Center tower and then two huge steel and glass structures reduced to a monstrous pile of rubble.

On September 10, we were all going about our business as usual. We were griping and complaining about our government. We were picking up our kids from school and taking them to ballgames and ballet lessons. We were too busy with a million things on our to-do lists and, if we'd stopped and admitted it, life was good. On September 11, our lives changed forever.

My first reaction to the terrorist attack was to flash back to those war times during my early childhood. That little mountain town of Deer Lodge, Montana, where I grew up was perhaps one of the safest places in the country. It sits placidly in a wide valley high in the mountains. At that time, it had a population of about 4,000 people. Men refined zinc, copper, manganese, and other metals in blast furnaces at the Anaconda Company where Dad worked. There they ladled the raw metal into molds to form ingots that were shipped out for manufacturing.

During the war years, most of the raw metal went to make the machines of war—jeeps, tanks, bombs, and all the other weapons needed to defend our country. Because metal produced at this smelter was essential to the war effort, the men who worked there were exempt from military duty. But exempt or not, they were as much "called to duty" as the men in uniform.

Dad worked seven days a week and hauled men twenty-four miles each way to and from the smelter. He worked day shift, night shift, and afternoon shift (swing shift) in two-week rotations. It seemed to me that my brothers and I spent much of those years tip-toeing around the house because "Daddy has to sleep."

Our family life formed around his rigid work schedule. Sometimes we ate our big meal at noon because "Daddy has to leave for swing shift right after we eat." Sometimes, when he was on night shift, he would sit at the kitchen counter with one work boot in his hand, looking almost too tired to put it on. Much of the time, it seemed as if he came and went like a wraith in the night. It was a tough, exhausting time not only for our family but also for all of America—for the soldiers in combat and for all those who "stayed by the stuff." Those were days of exhaustion and fear.

World War II was a long time ago, and looking back we gain a new perspective. We can see that God was with us and helped us, and after a while there came a cessation of war. The boys, turned into men by the horrors they had seen, came home and seemingly life went on as before. But we know now that life did not go on as before. Those fighting men have grown old, and even now when the few who remain talk of what they saw in combat, tears well up in their eyes, they choke up, and they cannot continue speaking.

Over time our nation grew fat and contented, and we thought no one could ever sneak up on us again and cause mass destruction. We thought we had it all figured out . . . until that awful summer day when tall buildings melted into their basements and killed more people than even the wartime attack on Pearl Harbor. On that day fear was driven through our hearts like a frozen sword. It was, and is, the raw jagged fear of not knowing what will come next.

We are forever changed, both as a nation and as individuals. Every time something goes bump in the night—or even in the daylight—we jump. We jump if it is another unexplained plane crash or white powder in an envelope or someone aboard a plane with a shoe bomb or a sniper randomly killing people. And even while we sing "Amazing Grace" or "God Bless America," somewhere in the secret recesses of our minds, we wonder where God is. We wonder if God really knows what is happening. We wonder if he cares.

Perhaps we can learn from history—the history of the way in which he has always cared for those who put their trust in him—our hearts will be comforted. God cares. God has always cared, and he doesn't want us to be afraid. He wants to be our help in a time of trouble and uncertainty.

A few words from the Holy Book are:

The LORD is good, a refuge in times of trouble.
He cares for those who trust in him (Nahum 1:7).

This message is not that there will be no trouble; it is that there will be a refuge in time of trouble. We can count on it.

When we pass through a troubled time, there will be a refuge for our souls. Such a refuge is incomprehensible in our imaginings. That's because we don't need the information now. But if such a fearful time comes to us, understanding will come to us as well, and we will see a way through our fear.

A favorite poem of mine speaks to this "not-knowing" state of our life:

At the Gate of the Year

I said to the man who stood at the gate of the year:
"Give me a light that I may tread safely into the unknown."
And he replied: "Go out into the darkness and put your
 hand into the Hand of God.
That shall be to you better than light and safer than a
 known way."
So I went forth, and finding the Hand of God, trod gladly
 into the night.
And he led me towards the hills and the breaking of day.
   —Minnie Louise Harkins 1875–1957

4

Puppies Under the House

I couldn't have been more than three years old when I discovered puppies under the house. Before Glen was born, Mom, Daddy, and I lived in Opportunity in a tiny two-room house that sat on blocks on top of the ground. There was no basement—I don't even know if there was skirting around the bottom of the house. The floors in that house must have been frigid in winter. It wasn't much of a place to live, but it was a whole lot better than one of Mom and Dad's previous houses. That had been an old icehouse located on the farm where my uncle worked. Mom and Dad cleaned out the sawdust used to insulate the ice from melting and put cardboard on the walls to make the place clean.

Mom begged Dad to build a fence around an area at the icehouse home so I would have a place to play. He was busy and didn't get to it. One day, I crossed a bridge—just a plank across an irrigation ditch—to visit my cousins who lived on the other side. In the water at one end of the plank was a rusty old tin can with minnows swimming in and out of it. I don't know if I was intrigued by the tiny fish or if I was just careless, but I fell into the ditch filled with rushing water. I screamed, and the adults came running. When they got to me, they knew I had been all the way under the water, as the hat I was wearing was soaking wet. I had not been completely swept away simply because I had grabbed a wild rose bush—prickles and all—and was hanging on for dear life. Dad built the fence that day.

Shortly after this, we moved to Opportunity—the house where we lived when Glen was born. Mom was a superb cook, and the little house was filled with the scent of cinnamon and homemade bread and vegetable soup. She would make noodles by mixing flour and eggs, and then she'd roll the dough out into a big sheet. With a kitchen knife, she'd cut the dough into strips and hang them up—probably on coat hangers—to dry. Then she'd boil a chicken and make chicken noodle soup. I loved it. I would eat my food with one hand on the serving bowl so no one would take it away until I'd had all I wanted.

I wanted to cook too, so one day when Mom's attention was diverted, I crawled up on the kitchen table, took down a stoneware crock that had been sitting on the window ledge, and broke a dozen eggs into it. Oh, those yellow yolks floating in the crock were so beautiful, just like sunflowers blooming in the meadow.

* * *

We had a red cocker spaniel named Trixie. She was a prolific breeder of pups of all kinds and colors, and she was my buddy. Well, Trixie went under the house and delivered a litter of pups. Gramma Cole came to visit and decided she wanted to see the pups. It meant someone had to crawl under the house, and because I was the smallest, I was elected to go.

I squirmed and wiggled my way under and discovered, to my great delight, that not only were there about half a dozen pups, but they also had their eyes open. When I wiggled my way out and delivered my news, there was quite a bit of doubt about whether those pups could possibly have their eyes open so soon. So somehow my grandmother wiggled her way in—at least part way—and wiggled out backward (she couldn't turn around) to confirm that indeed the pups had their eyes open.

It wasn't long until the pups came out to frolic in the early spring weather. Soon some of them were in the house and in the kitchen. Mom's faithful Maytag washing machine was tucked back of the door that led outside the house. In addition to the fearsome wringer that could catch your hand or your hair and pull it in, those old Maytag washers had a gearshift knob (used to stop or start the washing action) and a drain hose with a nozzle. The nozzle hooked onto the rim around the edge of the machine's tub. On this day, when the pups were indoors, there was a piece of cheesecloth hanging from the nozzle. One of the pups caught his teeth in it and couldn't get loose. I thought it was the funniest thing I had ever seen in my three years.

At least one of the pups was black and white. I named him Bull because he looked like the bull in the neighbor's pasture. One day, I tucked as many of the pups as I could into my wicker doll buggy and tried to cover them with a blanket to take them for a ride. However, it's impossible to cover a squirming mass of puppies and keep them in a carriage. The ride didn't last long.

Daddy and I fed the pups outdoors. We put an old tin pie plate on a block of wood, and I tried to dig the food out of a can. It was really stiff stuff, and the pups kept getting into it and eating what I managed to scrape onto the plate before I could finish dishing it out and setting it down for them. We finally got them fed.

One day I decided to sew. Everyone else in the family sewed, so I wanted to sew too. I climbed up to reach the pineapple-shaped, pink, crocheted pincushion that had blue taffeta showing through the holes. I think the pincushion was stuffed with coffee, because when I think of it, I can almost smell it. I removed a needle—it must have been threaded—from the pincushion. Holding the straight pins in my mouth just as Mom always did, I proceeded to sew the legs of my pajamas together—straight across both legs. Mom was pretty surprised when she tried to stuff me into those pajamas that night.

That house had no indoor bathroom facilities. I used a potty chair also painted brown (what an interesting choice of color for children's furniture) to match the crib. Mom and Daddy had to take a footpath to the outhouse.

Bath time was interesting. One evening Dad got the washtub down, put it in the middle of the kitchen floor, and filled it with warm water. Dad was more than six feet tall, so he just about had to fold himself into a knot to sit in that washtub. I remember him getting in with his underwear on. I just couldn't understand that.

"Daddy, you're wearing your underpants," I told him, as if he didn't know. To the day he died Dad was a very modest man. I remember him telling me then, "Well, you won't leave so I can take them off." He laughed, and I guess I finally got the message and left.

I'm pretty sure it was while we lived at this house that Mom and Dad played a trick on each other. They had been at a gathering where there had been a lot of fun and eating and talking. Mom wanted to take me home and put me to bed as it was getting late, but Dad kept talking and talking. Finally, she decided to pack me up, put me in the pickup truck they always drove, and take me home. She figured Dad could find his own way home.

When she approached the driveway, she slowed to turn into the road to the house. She drove just a little beyond the house to a parking area. She unloaded me and my gear and headed to the house. When she got there she found the door standing open, but the air coming from the house was warm. That meant the door could not have been open very long or the interior of the house would have been as cold as the outside.

She was a little alarmed at that point, but not as alarmed as she would be a moment later when a male voice said, "It's a shame you wouldn't wait for a fellow." It was my dad. When he saw she was leaving him, he rushed outside and climbed up on the running board (we had them in those days) and crouched down behind the spare tire for the short ride home. When she slowed to turn into the driveway, he jumped off and ran to the house. He didn't even have time to close the door. I'm not sure what they said to each other at that point, but I don't think we ever left anyone behind after that.

* * *

While we lived in that house, a neighbor lady, Mom, and I decided to make a super-duper snowman. The snow in Montana is usually a dry powdery stuff that I call "puffed snow." Usually, there is not enough moisture content to pack it sufficiently for making snowballs or a snowman. But this day it was wet and packed well into wonderful balls. We began a little bit back from where we wanted the snowman to stand and rolled the snowball toward the location.

We got the first one in place, and it was a monster. Then we backed up and rolled another one. When we got to the first one, we had a second huge snowball that was too big for the three of us to lift. As we stood there pondering our dilemma, I piped up, "Let's cut it in half." And that's just what we did. Soon we had a real three-tiered snowman with coal eyes and nose. (I don't think we used a carrot for his nose. We probably used a stick. Carrots were food, and we didn't waste food on snowmen.)

Not too long afterward, this same neighbor lady became ill. We went to see her once during her illness. I was so uncomfortable. It was as if she was living in some other person's emaciated, sick body. I couldn't understand it at all. She was way too young, but soon she died and never came again to roll snowballs with me.

I suppose what I learned from living in that little house was that it doesn't matter what you have. We had almost nothing. Since then I've seen some pretty humble homes in various places in the world: homes with mud floors and mud walls tucked under thatched roofs; homes that are merely shops with tiny rooms in the back where a dozen people live; homes that are boats given to some kind of industry; homes that are just sheds. I know now that what matters more than the physical house is that the home has a roof of love providing safe shelter for the family who lives there. What matters most is that the four walls of the home provide a haven of tenderness and understanding to keep out the sorrow and pain that inevitably come to all of us. Life will happen. Sometimes it brings the unfathomable loss of a friend, sometimes an unforgettable meal, and sometimes it just brings puppies under the house.

5

A New Home

By 1942 Mom and Dad could no longer cram their expanding family into the rented two-room house, so they decided to buy a house. They first looked in Anaconda. Living near the smelter, as other workers did, would make getting to work easier for Dad. However, because Gramma Cole lived in Deer Lodge, she would be available to help with us kids when needed. Mom and Dad decided that Deer Lodge, twenty-four miles north, would be a better choice.

There happened to be a small two-bedroom bungalow on a half-acre on Kentucky Street. This was the "west side" of town, which meant across the river and the railroad tracks from the main part of town. They bought the place—for $1,750. No, that is not the down payment, and no, it is not a typo. That's what they paid for the entire half-acre lot with house and sheds. Even then, they were so poor they had to borrow the down payment from Gramma.

The house was white clapboard on the lower half and brown shingles on the upper half with white window sashes. It had a front porch with about eight steps leading down to a small hill with five or more steps leading further down to the level part of the lawn. There were wide seats on either side of the porch. If you kicked those seats with your feet, it made an awesome noise.

There was latticework from the level of the porch floor to the ground, and there was a small door at the side for access under the porch. Once in a while we kids would venture under the porch to look around. The underside was full of spider webs, and there lived the biggest garden spiders I have ever seen in my life. Legs included, they were about two inches across. They had a brownish hump for a body. My skin still crawls just thinking about them.

The lot was full of trees and bushes. There must have been a dozen or more Aspen trees in the front yard, and there were huge clumps of lilac bushes. Bit by bit, Dad cut them down and exposed the yard to the brilliant Montana sun.

In back of the house was a jumble of old buildings. A woodshed—also painted brown—was only feet from the back door. Inside it was a coal bin and a wood storage area. When coal was delivered, the truck would dump it down a chute through a window and into the black interior of the bin. I can still remember the sound of it sliding down the chute. I loved to go into that old shed. It smelled of coal dust and the pine logs Dad had cut and brought down from the hills.

At some point, Dad built a fenced area just outside the window where the deliverymen dumped the coal. He filled the fenced-in area with about two feet of sand. Perhaps we had stopped using coal by then, because I never remember another delivery. We often played there in the sand—penned in, I guess.

The property also had a one-car garage—or a one-pickup garage, as it would be in our case. There had been a fire in the garage long before our time, and the walls were black and charred. Someone had tacked up cardboard to cover the charred wood. It may have hidden the blackened soot, but the smell of that charred wood seeped through the cardboard and into my memory. There it remains to this day, along with the smell of coal dust and stacked firewood.

There was one other low building that was a faded red. It probably had been a workshop, though my memory of its use was as a chicken house—a chicken house that once kept the meanest barred-rock rooster on earth. If you merely walked by the fence in front of the chicken house, he'd fly at it and become eighteen inches of pure fury. It probably didn't help that we knew we could upset him if we dragged a stick along the fence.

We once had a mother hen with a bunch of fluffy yellow chicks. Glen was a toddler then, and when Mom heard him laughing, she came to investigate. There he was with the hose, soaking that poor hen. She was frantically trying to cover the baby chicks with her sodden wings. She survived, and so did the chicks.

My first memory of the inside of our new house was that it had a bathroom with a humungous white claw-foot bathtub and a flushing toilet. Wow! First class for sure! In the kitchen was a massive cast-iron cook stove that took up a good portion of the floor space. At first the Round Oak stove burned wood, but later on Dad converted it to gas.

The ceilings in the kitchen were at least ten feet tall. The floor was black and white squares printed on linoleum. Shelves had been built into what had been a doorway on an end wall. Next to the doorway shelves was another door that led to a pantry. Mom put the kitchen table against the wall between those two doors. When we wanted to eat there, we had to raise heavy leaves on either side of the table. Heavy-duty hardware snapped into place to hold up a leaf on either side. Spread out, the table could easily accommodate our family.

Inside the pantry was a shelf that served as a work surface for food preparation. Above the shelf were more shelves, where we stored everything needed for Mom to create her wondrous baked goods. I remember sneaking in there, climbing on the shelf, and taking down the brown sugar to eat it right from the airtight jar where she stored it to keep it from going rock hard in Montana's dry climate. Always there was the smell of spices in the pantry, and in the fall, the smell of curing sauerkraut that Dad made after harvesting cabbage.

In the floor of the pantry was a trap door that led to a tiny cellar. The house had no basement. To get into the cellar you had to climb down a makeshift ladder. The cellar itself was about ten feet by ten feet and had dirt walls. The only thing of any interest or value we ever found down there was a broken wooden serving tray. Dad repaired it, and I still have it in my home and use it frequently. There was also a brass oil-burning lamp that he retrieved, polished, and wired for electricity.

Just off the kitchen was a tiny eating area. Windows with multiple panes of glass ran all around the room and opened inward. It was light and bright, but because the windows leaked air, it could be very cold in that room. When all five of us sat at the "dining room" table, it was a tight fit. Dad sat at one end of the table, and Mom sat at the other end. Glen and Ray sat with their backs to the window, and I sat across from them. The table was small enough that I could annoy them by kicking them without stretching too much and drawing attention to my actions.

Also in the kitchen was a door that led into a tiny bedroom known as the "back room." It had a lean-to roof and little insulation. In winter that room felt like someone had left the backdoor open to the North Pole. Mom and Dad slept in there, as the house had only two bedrooms. Just outside the door to the bedroom sat the refrigerator, and next to that a wood box that Dad kept full of wood for heating and cooking. He made the wood box and then made a cover from a large flat board and painted a checkerboard on it. One of my greatest joys was to climb inside the wood box when it was emptied and cleaned and pull the checkerboard lid over the opening to hide for a time. It was my special place.

The living room also had a wood-burning stove with a shiny two-toned brown enamel finish. There was a door in the front for loading in wood. The door had an isinglass window so you could see the level of the flame inside. (Isinglass is made from sheets of mica.) There was another door below the first where the ashes fell into a pan that could be removed for emptying. It was anything but an airtight stove, and ashes were a constant problem. Emptying them was a daily task. Mom or Dad would shovel out the ashes and take them outside to deposit in a heap. They were probably added to the garden soil in spring.

Once, when Ray was very little, he went out to play and stuck his hand in the hot ashes that had just been put out in the snow. While it was an awful accident and his skin was blistered, he had no scarring from it.

In the beginning the living room floor was covered with linoleum. But it was horribly worn, so Dad soon pulled it up and refinished the soft pine floor underneath. Then Mom and Dad purchased an overstuffed sofa and chair. The two pieces were maroon-colored mohair with wood trim on the front. They also purchased a small maroon-colored wool area rug, and Mom hung patterned draperies with a predominantly maroon floral pattern. A Philco radio that stood on the floor and looked like a piece of furniture and a couple of ancient lamps completed the room. The living room was called the "front room," and it served as a playroom, music room, family gathering room, and sometimes a sick room.

The front bedroom belonged to us kids—all three of us. The floor was also soft pine and not in the best condition. I learned the hard way that it wasn't wise to scoot across the floor. It took a long time to remove the splinters from my backside. The window in this room and the matching one in the living room were large and could be raised only about two feet. The two feet above the large pane of glass was clear leaded glass.

In the beginning, Glen had a cot on one side of the room and I had a single bed on the other side. When Ray was born, he slept in that old brown crib placed at the end of the room, the one nearest the warmth of the woodstove in the living room. It was probably a good thing to have the baby near the warmth.

This baby, born in September when the nights were getting very crisp, weighed only five pounds at birth. He stayed tiny for quite some time. Even when he could crawl and Mom had put him in a long white sleep garment that trailed behind him, he was so little they called him "Sweet Pea," after the character in the Popeye comic strip.

I'm sure we kids did just about everything other kids did, both good and bad, and we thought up some of our own mischief. I remember chewing a huge wad of bubble gum, taking it out and sticking it to one wall of our bedroom, and then stretching it across the room to stick it to the other wall. I would have several strands stretching across the room.

Later on when we were a little older, Glen and Ray moved into a big, old-fashioned brass bed placed in that same room. I still had my single bed, and it sat crossways at the end of their bed. After we were all in bed, I would get up, crouch on the high brass foot of the bed, and taunt my brothers. Sometimes it took a little while, but they would always yell for our parents, saying I was bugging them. I could hear my dad's chair scrape on the floor as he pushed it back to stand up. At that point, I would fall over backward into my own bed and in one smooth motion turn myself to the wall and pull the covers up. Then I would breathe slowly and evenly. I'd hear Dad say, "She's asleep. She's not bothering you. Now go to sleep."

When we woke on cold winter mornings, it would be to the sound of the stove door in the living room being opened. There stood Mother, skinny and in her nightgown, making a fire. In one of those "don't try this at home" moments, she would first make kindling by taking a stick of wood and wedging it between herself and the stove in such a way that it would not slip. Then, with one hand on the handle of a butcher knife and the other wrapped all the way around the blade, she would cut and pry up strips from the piece of wood to make more or less of a K-shaped kindling the fire could grasp easily. Soon she had a roaring fire going, and then it was time for us to get up. We would take our clothes and lay them on top of the stove to warm them. Depending on how hot the fire was and how long we left them there, we often scorched them and had to go to school with brown stripes across our clothing.

That house, too, soon became too small for all of us. It was time to make a change. But what change?

6

Christmas Came Early

One of the Christmases I will never forget was the year Santa came early to our house. It happened like this.

At the zinc casting plant in the Anaconda Company smelter, men were rotated on a two-week schedule between day shift, afternoon shift, and night shift (commonly called graveyard shift). At certain times during the rotation, Dad would have something called a "long change," where he had a couple days off before rotating to the next shift. Those were great times, and when they happened in summer, we would often get away to camp and fish. But there was also a "short change" in the rotation. Dad would come home, sleep a few hours, and be headed back to work on "the hill," which is what we called the smelter.

Well, one year one of those short changes happened right at Christmas. While Dad earned double pay working on Christmas Day, which was good for the family economics, the down side was that he would be gone both Christmas Eve and most of Christmas Day. My parents debated what to do about our Christmas celebration.

* * *

This happened during the time when we three kids were still sleeping in the same room. One morning Glen got up to use the bathroom. It was December 23. Soon he tiptoed back and whispered, "Gwenie, Santa has been here."

Always the practical one, I replied, "No, he hasn't. It isn't even Christmas Eve yet."

"Yes, he has," Glen whispered. "Come see."

So I got out of bed and went to the living room, and he was right. There were presents all over the place. Some of them were wrapped and some weren't. We didn't know what to think. We didn't know what to do.

Our parents knew they had just pulled off the greatest Christmas surprise ever. They had been awake in their room waiting for us to discover it. Soon they appeared, and we all celebrated Christmas a whole two days before anyone else did. It was a Christmas I'll never forget.

There is another Christmas that stands out in my memory. When this Christmas happened, our world had been at war for a number of long, frightening years. Supplies had become less and less available. Mother's books of ration coupons would barely stretch to buy food and gasoline and a few pieces of clothing that couldn't be made on her little sewing machine. If you didn't have the right coupon for the item, you didn't get to buy it.

So Mom saved her coupons for shoes and coats and food, though many times she even made our coats. She and Dad canned as much food as he could grow. He hunted and prayed for wild game (deer, elk, antelope, game birds, trout, and even bear) for meat for the family. The problem was that even if Mom had coupons, there were many things she could not buy because they were simply not available.

This particular year when it was almost Christmas, Mom and Dad had a dilemma. Their three little kids were looking forward to Christmas, but there were no toys available. So, being ever resourceful, they decided to manufacture their own. They fashioned a dollhouse for me by putting two wooden orange crates together.

Since no one has seen an orange crate in about a million years, let's talk about it for a moment. First of all, the need for orange crates. Oranges were once a great delicacy. It was a big treat to get an orange in your Christmas stocking. I don't remember oranges being much of a delicacy for me, so I assume they were more readily available when I was a child. I do remember that on Christmas Eve we would hang our stockings on a coat hanger on a doorknob. We didn't have a fireplace where we could hang them. And we didn't have fancy stockings.

I hung one of my long, brown cotton everyday school stockings—the kind that were held up by a garter belt—on the hanger and fastened it there with a clothespin. My brothers hung their socks on the same wire hanger. They probably thought I was trying to cheat them, as my stocking was long and their socks were only ankle length. On Christmas morning, however, theirs always looked full, and mine just had gifts down in the foot. Anyway, when I got an orange in my stocking, I felt gypped. I wanted candy—and lots of it.

Oranges were shipped in wooden crates that were about three feet long, eighteen inches wide, and a foot deep. The crate was divided in the middle by a solid wooden board, probably to add strength and to divide the precious oranges from crushing each other. Those crates were good for lots of things. You could stack them up for shelves and use them to store things. You could make a dressing table by placing two of them end up about three feet apart, topping them with a board, and attaching a fabric skirt all around. What more could you want than a dressing table with shelves under the skirt? You could easily break the side slats of the crate to use for kindling. You could take the ends and middle of the crates and make birdhouses and many other wonderful inventions. You could attach wheels and a handle to the crate and make a rough kind of scooter.

This Christmas, however, two crates fastened side by side became a dollhouse. There were four rooms—two up and two down. Mother wallpapered the rooms with samples from wallpaper books. She fitted the floor with scraps of fabric and even crocheted a little oval bedside rug. Dad built a dollhouse-sized sofa and covered it with gray-green mohair. He also built a tiny bed. Mother made a striped mattress complete with tufting. She also made sheets, a quilt, a bedspread, and a pillow sham.

Somewhere they found or purchased a few pieces of plastic furniture. There was a desk with a center drawer that opened and a Duncan Phyfe-styled table and four chairs. The only problem was that all the furniture was plastic and all the same color—maroon. The whole thing was very primitive, but I still have the sofa and the little bed with all its fixings. I treasure them as if they were toys handcrafted for a princess.

The boys were not left out. Dad made a wooden jeep for each one. He perfectly recreated every detail of the jeeps in wood and painted them dark green. You see, even in that remote area of Montana, far from fighting and bloodshed of World War II, jeeps and the implements of war were a part of our daily conversation. Dad also made a truck with a crane on the back. The crane actually had a pulley and a crank handle to hoist things. Overall, it was about a foot tall. It seems there might have been one or two other vehicles in the collection.

The only problem Dad had with his vehicles was that he could not find wheels for them. I'm not sure why they were not available, but there were no wheels to be found. He didn't have a lathe to make wooden wheels, so he solved the problem by casting metal wheels at the zinc casting plant. They were about three inches in diameter, and when the four of them were applied to a truck or jeep, you could hardly lift the toy off the floor.

These handmade, homemade toys were very crude. But today I am humbled when I think of how these two devoted parents, who had little money and little time (since Daddy was working seven days a week for the war effort), stayed up nights to be sure we kids had a wonderful Christmas. I love them for it.

All of our Christmases were pretty much handmade—even after the war. One year, Mom knit me a two-piece pink dress with angora trim. It was beautiful. Another year she took an old Alaskan lamb fur coat—real fur—and made a teddy bear for Ray. And there were homemade game boards, clothes, and ride-on toys—including a little scooter you could steer that had red reflectors on the back for Glen.

Sometime after Thanksgiving, out came the ingredients to make fruitcakes for our consumption and to give as gifts. Over the years, Mom tried all kinds of fruitcakes. I liked the ones that were mostly fruit and nuts and not much batter. Well, Mom mixed and stirred and put the batter in bread pans. After she baked the fruitcakes she wrapped them in cheesecloth, then in kitchen towels, and then, because we were a tee-total household, she poured vinegar rather than wine on the wrappings to keep the cakes moist.

Believe it or not, even with the vinegar they were not too bad. Okay, I confess that fruitcake was not my favorite—until Mom discovered something called a Lane Cake. It was a delicious three-layer cake with a cooked filling of candied cherries, nuts, and coconut sandwiched between the layers and spread on the top. Yum! Many people first learned of the cake from the novel *To Kill a Mockingbird* by Harper Lee, when Miss Maudie promised to make one for old Mr. Avery. When it was finished, Scout declared that Miss Maudie's cake was "so shiny, it made me tight."

Grandma Cole was always a part of our Christmas, and she contributed heavily to our handmade gifts. She was an amazing lady. Unschooled as far as books go, she could create wonders with her hands. Almost every Christmas of my life I got a new pair of wool mittens from her. They always fit. Sometimes they were one solid color—blue, red, or black. Sometimes they looked as though they had been made from scraps of yarn—and they probably had. She knit them seamless on six double-pointed needles. One Christmas she made me a long warm scarf of multi-colored yellow, brown, and white variegated yarn. I still have it.

She had another favorite gift—a tree ornament. Grandma Cole had been raised in the South. One of her favorite stories was about chewing tobacco with her friends and then seeing who could spit the farthest. It was an awful habit, but chew she did until the day she died. She didn't chew a plug of tobacco but used snuff. She (and we) improperly called it "snooce." It came in little round cans that were about two inches high. Somewhere along the way, Grandma discovered that a silver dollar would just fit in the bottom of those snuff cans. So she would decorate them with Christmas wrap and fit them with a cord for hanging. Then she would place a silver dollar into the bottom. Sometimes she would tuck other tiny treats in there, but more often than not, it would just be a silver dollar.

We didn't save the dollars because they were silver. Silver dollars were a main means of exchange in Montana. I rarely saw a paper dollar until I was grown. You could go to the grocery store for some little thing and come out weighed down with silver. Montanans liked money that made noise, and they loved their silver dollars. Anyway, we usually spent the money Gramma gave us the first chance we got, and we enjoyed every bit of it. And it didn't matter at all that our gift from Gramma Cole came in a "snooce" can.

At our house, we wouldn't think of buying a Christmas tree. Dad always brought us a Christmas tree from the woods. Often he and Mom would come home from hunting, and while they hadn't gotten any game, they would have found the perfect tree. Sometimes the trees were a little misshapen—nothing like the perfectly formed Christmas lot trees we find today. If our tree was a little bare in one spot, Dad would bore a hole in the trunk and insert a branch the right size. Sometimes that limb wasn't too sturdy, so he'd rig a wire to hold it in place. The only kind of Christmas tree stand I can ever remember having was two pieces of wood nailed together in a cross and attached to the bottom. Of course, the upper part of the wooden cross had to have little blocks of wood attached at either end to make the stand level.

Mom was in charge of decorating the tree, and because she was a perfectionist, it was quite a challenge to do it right. First of all, the light bulbs—often blue—had to have a reflector on them. Mom had two kinds. One was a foil shape that looked like a flower, and the other was an industrial-strength pierced metal star that could injure your fingers if handled carelessly. She would take a light bulb in one hand, insert the screw end of the bulb through the hole in the reflector, and then screw it into the socket. The result was that the light from the bulb was magnified to about two-inches across. It was lovely.

The glass balls came after all the lights with reflectors were on the tree. These were always blue and silver. Gramma Cole had some German-handcrafted ornaments that were wonderful, but she kept them at her house. All of this decorating was the easy part.

Then we had to put on the icicles. These icicles were not the float-away plastic kind you might find now; they were made of tinfoil and were quite heavy. Everyone had icicles on their trees, but some people just stood back and threw them at the tree. Not us. Mom insisted that every icicle be placed on the branch one by one, every quarter of an inch apart. It was such a tedious task that I now wonder if it took us the entire Christmas season to put them on. The end result was stunning—a blue and silver tree with perfectly placed icicles.

When Christmas was over, we had to carefully lift all those icicles off the tree, put them on cardboard, and then wrap them in tissue paper to be saved for another year. We wasted nothing. Who cared that next year the icicles were a little bent? When we finished taking everything off the tree, there were still a few stray icicles here and there.

Homemade mittens, homemade toys, silver dollars in snuff cans, love, warmth, plenty to eat, happiness, joy—what more could a child want?

Lane Cake

Cake
3½ cups cake flour
2 teaspoons cream of tartar
2 teaspoons baking soda
¼ teaspoon salt
1 cup milk, at room temperature
1 teaspoon pure vanilla extract
2 sticks (½ pound) unsalted butter, softened
2 cups sugar
8 large egg whites, at room temperature

Filling
12 large egg yolks
1½ cups sugar
1½ sticks (6 ounces) unsalted butter, melted and cooled
1½ cups (6 ounces) finely chopped pecans
1½ cups (10½ ounces) finely chopped raisins
1½ cups freshly grated coconut
½ cup bourbon
1½ teaspoons pure vanilla extract
¼ teaspoon salt

1. Preheat the oven to 325° F. Butter three nine-inch round cake pans and line the bottoms with parchment paper. Butter the paper and dust with flour, tapping out the excess.

2. Sift the flour, cream of tartar, baking soda, and salt into a medium bowl. In a small pitcher, combine the milk and vanilla. In a large bowl, beat the butter on medium speed until creamy. Slowly add the sugar and beat until light and fluffy, scraping down the sides of the bowl. On low speed, alternately add the dry ingredients and

the milk in three batches. Beat the batter until smooth, scraping down the sides of the bowl as necessary.

3. In another bowl, using clean beaters, beat the egg whites until they form soft peaks. Stir one-third of the egg whites into the cake batter to lighten it. Using a rubber spatula, fold in the remaining egg whites until no white streaks remain.

4. Pour the batter into the cake pans and smooth the tops. Tap the pans lightly on a work surface to release any air bubbles. Bake the cakes on the middle and lower racks of the oven for about thirty minutes, shifting the pans halfway through, until the tops spring back when pressed lightly and a toothpick inserted in the center comes out with a few moist crumbs attached. Let cool in the pans for five minutes, and then invert the cakes onto a wire rack to cool completely. Peel off the paper.

5. In a large saucepan, combine the egg yolks and sugar and stir until smooth. Add the melted butter and cook over moderate heat, stirring, until thick enough to coat the back of a spoon (about six minutes). Do not let it boil. Stir in the pecans, raisins, and coconut and cook for about one minute. Add the bourbon, vanilla, and salt and let cool to lukewarm.

6. Place a cake layer on a serving plate, right side up, and spread with 1¼ cups of the filling. Repeat with a second cake layer and another 1¼ cups of filling. Top with the last cake layer and frost the cake with the remaining filling. Let the cake cool completely before serving.

Make Ahead
Refrigerate the cake in a tightly covered container for up to one week. Serve at room temperature.

Accessed at: http://www.foodandwine.com/recipes/lane-cake, September 9, 2015.

7

Trains

World War II ended when I was seven years old, but both before and after that time, thousands of troops moved back and forth across the country. They moved not on airplanes but on trains—troop trains. Because our little town was one of the main stops for the Milwaukee Railroad, long troop trains would pull into the station for complete servicing. Workers cleaned the trains and put ice on board for refrigeration purposes. We could always tell troop trains from other trains, as the paint on the cars was a dull khaki color.

The military personnel usually stayed on board while the train was being serviced at the station. There was, however, a small canteen operated by local people where troops could refresh themselves with coffee, cold drinks, and homemade cookies. When it was open, soldiers would get off and mill about the station. Because we lived on the "west side" of town—the "other side of the tracks"—we usually saw the troop trains when they arrived.

Workers harvested the ice during the long, bitter cold Montana winters, when the ice on the local ponds would freeze two- to three-feet thick. They packed the cut ice in sawdust and stored the blocks in icehouses until needed in spring and summer. Often when we were walking home from school or from swim lessons on hot days, we would find chunks of crystal-clear ice on the ground with the sawdust still sticking to them. We would brush off the sawdust and suck on the ice all the way home. The only problem was that most of the chunks were too big for our little mouths. The ice was so hard that even smacking them down on the ground didn't break them into smaller pieces.

One time I was walking home and a troop train was sitting at the crossing. I had to wait for it to clear the track. A soldier leaned out the window of the train and waved a couple of letters in my face. "Little girl," he said, "would you mail these for me?" I stretched up as far as I could, and he leaned down as far as he could. I took his letters and mailed them. It was just a tiny action, a flash in time, the contact of two human lives. I still remember it. Times were different then, and no one thought anything about a little girl doing something like this for a stranger. It was just a kind gesture.

A few months after my youngest brother Ray was born, Mother was weary and in need of a rest. Her father had died that summer. Daddy was still working seven days a week at the smelter. Ray and Glen were only eighteen months apart in age, and I was just four. Mother had three children under the age of five and was virtually raising them alone because of the hours Daddy was putting in on his job.

Mother and Daddy decided that she should take the three of us kids to Washington State to visit her sister, Edith, who was married to Daddy's brother, Wayne. (Their five kids are my double cousins because of the sibling relationships of our parents.) The train we were taking was not a troop train, but it was loaded with military people just the same. I suppose if I were to see these military personnel today, they would seem very young in their khaki-colored uniforms, but as a child I stood in awe of them. These were soldiers. They were protecting our land from the enemy. They were our heroes, and we were grateful to them for their sacrifice.

They were just like my Uncle Hughlun and Uncle Hoy, Mother's brothers, who were serving in the army. Uncle Hoy became a career military man with the rank of major. He served far away in mysterious Africa. When Mom tried to explain what the end of the war would be like, she would say, "Uncle Hoy will come home, and we will be able to buy butter." It was a long, long time before Uncle Hoy came home, and just as long until we could buy butter.

We climbed aboard the train, and Mom found a pair of seats facing each other. She put Ray on the seat next to her, and Glen and I crawled up onto the opposite seat. She had food, toys, and everything one might need for a 600-mile train trip with three little ones. I don't know how she or anyone of that time managed travel with only cloth diapers, but she did.

At the end of the car was a desk where the conductor could do his paperwork. Mom saw that the desk wasn't being used, so she let Glen sit there and color in a brand new coloring book. He sat working with the same intense concentration he used for all his tasks—curly blond head bent over his work and tongue sticking out and moving back and forth as he carefully applied his chosen colors. He was totally absorbed in what he was doing when the door at the end of the car swung open and a conductor in a dark blue uniform and cap with silver-colored braid strode up to the desk.

"Whose kid is this?" he asked with annoyance.

"Mine," Mom answered.

"Why is he sitting here? This is my desk."

"I didn't know that," she said, "and he needed a place to color. Come here, Glen."

"No," the brusque conductor told her. "Let him be. I can use the one in the next car." He went striding out with the rolling gait that walking on a moving train causes.

It must have been an unpleasant experience for Mom. She was only about twenty-five at the time, was traveling alone with three very young children, and was tired. Night came, and she bedded us down to the best of her ability. Somehow Glen and I shared the double seat, Mom stretched out on the opposite seat, and the baby lay in a makeshift bed on the floor between us. It wasn't the most comfortable night.

In the morning, the train conductor—making another walk through his assigned cars—stopped for a moment beside our seat. Mom stirred and opened one eye. "I've had the toughest time keeping that kid covered up," he said as he pointed to Glen. Then we knew that all his huffiness was on the outside and sheltered a tender heart.

When we got to the farm where Edith and Wayne lived, we kids ate fresh strawberries from the patch that were drowned in cream from the family's cow. We smelled the roses that were in full bloom and rambled over old sheds. We giggled with our cousins long past our bedtime and tried to listen to the grownups' conversation through a grate in the floor. We played in the sunshine. One of the games we played was war. All kids played war in those days. My oldest boy cousin, Bob, had rigged a post in such a way that he could turn it from side to side and up and down. This was his anti-aircraft gun, and he attacked the enemy with an "ak-ak-ak-ak" sound. War was all around us. We breathed it. We lived with a constant low-grade fear that it would come to our town—to our neighborhood.

I remember being in our own back yard in Montana when I heard planes. Dad looked up and was instantly concerned. There, above our little mountain village, was a squadron of planes flying in formation. Dad's response to that sight ran like a shiver of fear through me. We didn't know whose planes they were. We didn't know if we should take cover. We listened for the town siren that would warn us of danger. Surely, the air wardens, whose job it was to warn us of impending danger from above, would sound the siren if there was danger. None came that day.

I remember blackout shades for night times and listening to the radio to see if we needed to cover the windows. I remember Mom explaining to me that we did not want the enemy to be able to see light and know there were houses down below. Truthfully, our little town of Deer Lodge was probably of little interest to them, but we didn't know that. Probably the smelter where Daddy worked so many days and hours would have been a prime target, but we didn't know that either. And so we lived with the constant sense of not knowing what would come next.

But back to our trip. After two or three weeks of resting in the soft summer air of western Washington, Mom was ready to start home. We had to go to Seattle to catch the train, and I remember there was a fair amount of concern about our being able to get on it. Military personnel had priority. The public had been advised not to travel, and *especially* not to travel with children. But Mom was a feisty one and traveled anyway. Now the challenge was to get us home. We would catch the train at King Street Station in Seattle.

Years later, when I lived in Seattle, I went several times to King Street Station. It did not seem the huge frightening place that it did that night when I was four years old and running to catch a train. Uncle Wayne had me by one hand and I don't know who had the other one, but I do remember the brass handrails and marble steps that are still in the station. I remember that my feet never touched those marble steps all the way down to the platform as the adults lifted me up and ran down the stairs. I remember the thick crowd of uniforms as military personnel tried to climb aboard, and I remember that someone finally cleared a path for a tiny lady and her brood.

* * *

The next day when we arrived home, someone—not Daddy, since he was at work—picked us up from the train and took us home. The house was immaculate. Dad had scrubbed and polished it from top to bottom, and on the table was a new pale blue vase, crammed with the first sweet peas of the season—my father's gift to his bride.

* * *

The Milwaukee Railroad was the lifeline of our little town, and a lifeline for our family. My Grandfather Cole had come to Montana—to Three Forks where Lewis and Clark had once walked and named the three rivers the Gallatin, the Madison, and the Jefferson—from North Carolina because he heard there was work to be had on the railroad. He was a carpenter and he did go to work for the railroad in Three Forks. It wasn't too long until he transferred to Deer Lodge, which had the largest shops for train repair between Minneapolis and Seattle. He worked there the rest of his life. With his job, came that wonderful lifetime railroad pass for himself, his wife, and his kids that allowed my grandmother to climb on a train and travel back to North Carolina.

While the railroad provided a livelihood for many in our town, at times it could also be the bane of our existence. Inevitably, if you were late to something or in a hurry, there would be a train on the tracks switching back and forth as cars were organized in order of their priority for delivery farther down the line. There was a small engine called a "switch engine" that hustled back and forth sorting the cars—across the only street from the west side of town where we lived to the east side of town where the businesses, schools, and churches were located.

All of the trains at that time were electric and connected to overhead lines by means of a carriage that made contact with the electricity. The switch engine did the same.

Since we lived only two blocks from the railroad and about six blocks from the roundhouse, when we went to bed at night, we could hear the freight cars banging together. One would think the noise would be unbearable, but we were used to it and it was kind of a comforting sound. On very cold nights, the sounds carried even more loudly through the air. Sometimes it seemed we might have a railroad line right next to the house.

There was another little oddity operated by the Northern Pacific Railroad, called "The Galloping Goose." I can barely remember it and I never rode on it. It operated between Deer Lodge and Butte for a short period of time, hauling workers and shoppers back and forth. Its sole function was to convey people between the two towns. Most Galloping Goose trains I've found in research looked a little different than what I remember. What I remember was more like a streetcar. A standard Galloping Goose looked like a combination bus/railcar.

I can still remember steam engines, although only barely. There was, for a time, a water tank on the Northern Pacific railroad in Deer Lodge, and only once do I remember seeing a train taking on water at that tank. I do, however, remember the huge steam engines we called "malleys." The correct spelling is mallet, even though the word is pronounced "malley."

Those old steam mallets were like fire-breathing dragons to us kids. If you were standing on the train platform when one rolled into the station you could feel the ground shake and smell burnt coal as steam poured from beneath the engine. The brakes screeched as the engineer applied the brakes and the train came to a halt. It was an awesome and somewhat frightening experience. In my head I knew the train would not jump the track, but in my heart I was afraid that it might.

One evening we three and Mom tagged along on Dad's fishing trip to the Little Blackfoot River. It's a wonder any of us survived those evening fishing trips as the mosquitoes tried to completely drain all our blood. Anyway, we were sitting—more like clinging to—the crushed rock—ballast—of the Northern Pacific Railroad's rail bed, ten feet from the tracks. Then we heard it coming. The steam mallet roared down the tracks at full speed, smoke belching from its stack and steam spewing from beneath it. The ground shook and we were sure we were doomed. I don't know if the engineer ever saw us, but we saw him—just feet above our heads—as the engine and a long freight train banged and screeched past us.

I miss railroads and railroad travel. I miss the smell of the burning coal. I miss the little depots with ticket men peering through brass grates and dispensing paper tickets. I miss the wood-burning stove that heated so many of those depots. I miss the heavy baggage carts wheeled out to claim the luggage, mail, and milk cans the train carried. I miss seeing conductors put down the little metal train stepstool and helping people off the train. I miss the conductor waving a lantern and yelling "Bord." I miss the express trains that didn't stop in our town but snagged the mail bag from a pole as the train hurtled past.

Although each era has its good things and its bad, and although I don't think I'd like to travel all the way across the United States in a train, I still miss everything about train travel.

8

The Great Remodel

I was getting older and as the only girl, I really needed a room of my own. Mom and Dad debated and talked and even went house hunting for a place for us to live nearer the smelter. I went on one of those excursions and I remember walking into a house for sale that had no electricity. The people who owned it were sitting inside with only a kerosene lantern. It was the spookiest place I had seen in my young life.

After much debate, one day Dad took a sledgehammer and went to the outside wall of the basement and broke a hole in the cement foundation. With that our total remodel of our existing home began. When I came home from school, I couldn't believe what was happening. By hand he shoveled wheelbarrow after wheelbarrow of dirt from beneath the house and piled it in the front yard until we had a mountain of soil in the front yard. It became the neighborhood playground.

After a while, Dad dug down to a level where there had been an old stream bed and there was a vein of almost pure gravel, just what he needed for the concrete work he would have to do. He shoveled the gravel into a pile by itself and washed it in preparation for combining it with sand and concrete.

Then he made forms and poured the foundation under the existing house foundation that was only about three feet tall. I'm not sure how he tied the house and the foundation together but sixty years later it is still standing and is still in one piece.

While all this was going on, there was one night of abject terror. It was February and Dad had excavated an area under the front of the house. Before he could get the forms in place and having just wheeled another load of dirt out of the basement, he heard a shushing sound and turned to see the existing foundation under the front of the house slide down and out of sight.

That night he couldn't sleep. He was sure the front of the house was going to collapse into the hole. It didn't, but he had a huge and heavy problem. First, he had to get rid of the old foundation that was now flat under the house. He solved the problem by breaking the concrete into pieces and burying it in the dirt that would soon become the basement floor. He did it all by hand not even using a jackhammer. That finished, he quickly built forms and poured concrete. Because it was so bitterly cold outside, a very real concern was that the concrete would freeze and later on would crumble. He covered the concrete on the outside of the house with old rugs and blankets and he kept a fire going night and day on the inside until the concrete cured. It worked and the concrete still stands, although that room, the one we called the "outside room" until recently was not finished.

There were to be four small rooms in the basement. One was a bedroom for the boys, one was a bedroom for me, and the third was the "fruit room." Mom canned everything she could get her hands on and it had to be stored somewhere where it would not freeze. It went into this little room filled with shelves. The fourth room was kind of an oversized hallway from which you could access all the other rooms. This is where Dad put a gas stove that kept the downstairs warm, and it also heated the upstairs, as heat would flow up the open staircase. There was a fan on the side of the stove and it was a great place to sit and dry my long strawberry blond hair.

There was one other feature in this room that didn't turn out as hoped. Dad built a kind of cupboard in the wall. If you opened the door of this cupboard, you looked into a cubbyhole with dirt walls extending under the back part of the house. (The excavation had stopped short of the dining area and back bedroom.) This is where he planned to store potatoes. The only problem was that the potatoes froze and became inedible.

Before we could move into these "digs" (literally) there was a lot of work to be done, and a lot of fun to be had, and even some sorrow. After all the concrete was poured, the basement still had that wet-concrete smell. It's interesting how often smells trigger memories for me. To this day, when I smell wet concrete, my mind flashes back to the basement. We kids moved down there before it was finished. To gain some privacy, we tacked blankets to the floor joists above and made little rooms for ourselves. At night, we would go into the area where the fruit room would soon be, get apples from a box stored there, and eat them. Then we would throw the cores under the bed. Sometimes there would a dozen cores in various stages of drying under the bed.

I said there was some sorrow during the construction. Sometime in the past, Dad had injured his back. I don't know when it happened, perhaps when he carried a large heavy upright piano into the house on his back. From time to time his muscles would spasm and he would have to go to bed until he got relief from the pain. Well, during this huge project, it happened again and he tried to keep going. He would lie on the floor trying to nail down baseboards to get our rooms finished.

This time, his back went into a spasm when he was working in the garden screening dirt to produce the rock-free, fine soil that grew masterpiece vegetables. One minute he was fine and the next the growth that had formed around a chip in his spinal column finally pinched off the nerve and sent him crawling into the house and into bed. This time his back didn't get better—not even when he rigged up a traction device by cutting a hole in the back of a boot, attaching a rope through it, feeding the rope through a pulley, and tying jugs of water on the end of the rope. He would put the boot on, lace it up, and lie down on the bed and let the weight pull his leg straight. It didn't help much.

The doctor came and first prescribed painkillers, then told him he had a ruptured disk and needed surgery. Perhaps he would even need a bone fusion in his spine. There was no place in western Montana where this could be done, and he simply wasn't going to be able to work until he had surgery.

Loaded up with painkillers, he was more than a little goofy. We kids stood by his bed and just watched him. This couldn't be happening to our tall strong daddy. Occasionally, he would rouse himself and say something so off the wall that we couldn't help but giggle. (One time he saw jugs of water all over the bedroom floor.) Then we'd feel bad that we had laughed at him.

The only solution for this problem was for he and Mom to go by train to Seattle where the surgery to remove a walnut-sized ruptured disk could be done at Providence Hospital. He had several sisters living in the area and Mom could stay with one of them. We three kids stayed with Grandma Cole for the three weeks and for once, we behaved ourselves.

We were so worried about our Daddy. We worried about us too. We knew Dad wasn't going to be able to work for at least three months. We didn't know how we were going to live without his income. It wasn't until later we realized what Mom had done for all of us. She had gone to officials at the Anaconda company, told them what had happened, explained what we needed, and got total coverage for the surgery and our living expenses.

* * *

Three weeks later when the big diesel engine pulling a train from Seattle roared into the Northern Pacific train station in Deer Lodge, it's bell ringing, the ground shaking under it's weight and motion, and the unmistakable smell of burned diesel fuel, my heart pounded. Even though I was older when Dad's back injury caused the trip to Seattle, I still was apprehensive on the train platform when one of those massive engines belched its way to where I stood and screeched to a stop with steam and smoke obliterating my view.

The door of the coach opened, the conductor stepped down, and put a little metal train stool down. I expected to see a hobbling sick man and a destitute-looking woman step from the train. Those two would be my parents. What greeted me instead blew my mind. There was Mom in a new coat and hat. She looked smashing! A very thin Daddy eased himself off the train. Things weren't as bad as I thought. We weren't going to starve—not if Mom could buy an outfit like that. We ran to them and hugged Mom hard, but weren't sure how to touch Daddy. We soon realized it was just Dad in a well-repaired body.

The coat and hat were the result of my aunts trying to pull a trick on Mom. They sent her to I. Magnin in Seattle to shop. She didn't understand what a high-end store I. Magnin was. There wasn't anything like it in Montana. But the laugh was on my aunts, as Mom found incredible sales and bought a number of things she truly needed. The next day, the aunts were ready to go shopping too.

The following three months at home were delightful. Dad was with us all day long—every day. Sometimes he would cook. Often he would make things in his shop. He talked to us and told us stories. We missed him when he was finally cleared to go back to the smelter where for a few more weeks he would push a broom around until the doctors released him to do the heavy work of the plant.

* * *

After a time, the house got finished and we three moved downstairs. We still only had one bathroom, and it was upstairs. We had to learn to share. I can't tell you how many times after dinner when we kids were supposed to do the dishes that Ray disappeared into that bathroom and locked the door and avoided dish detail.

So many things happened while we lived in that house. All three of us spent our childhood sheltered within its walls. Someone has said, "It takes a heap of living to make a house a home." There's a lot of truth in that worn-out old saying. It certainly took a heap of living for us five Ellises to make our house a home. But in the end, we look back with a lot of gratitude for the life we had.

9

Getting into Hot Water

Montana has sixty-one hot springs, most of which are in the western half of the state. I'm not a geologist, but the earth's crust must be pretty thin in some places in western Montana. We know that Yellowstone National Park, with all it's amazing thermal activity, located 215 miles directly south of Deer Lodge, is little more than the top of a huge volcano—one that geologists say could blow its top at any time in a super explosion.

The area around Deer Lodge is home to several hot springs. One amazing thermal feature is located about twenty miles from the house at a place called Warm Springs. The spring has formed a forty-foot mound of material that built up as the hot water overflowed for thousands of years. It's a process similar to the formation of stalactites and stalagmites in caves.

The mound is obvious in the wide, five-to-ten mile Deer Lodge Valley where everything is flat. It was once a meeting place for the Indian tribes who hunted white-tailed deer in the area. In summer the mound is not as spectacular as it is in winter when steam rises in a great cloud from its mouth. For the Indian tribes, it became a beacon, a rallying point for the hunting tribes. They called the springs *"It Soo-Ke En Car-Ne,"* meaning "The Lodge of the White-Tailed Deer," because it bore a striking resemblance to an Indian lodge with smoke ascending from it. Many white-tailed deer were drawn to the mound to lick the salty deposits and graze near the warm spring during the winter. From the name "The Lodge of the White-Tailed Deer," Deer Lodge took its name.

I've only been to the top of the mound a couple of times because the spring is within the confines of the state mental hospital. When I did go, I was overwhelmingly impressed with it. A short steep climb up the mound brings one to a Pergola someone built with a circular concrete hole in the center, and in that hole, hot water boils and bubbles like some ancient witch's cauldron.

There is another warm spring of water about forty miles in the other direction from this spring. I'm not sure where it exits the ground, but a warm stream of water flows through a field and finally pours over a cliff in a pounding shower of warm water. This spring has never been developed, so it was a totally informal place and probably a lot of local residents don't even know where the warm waterfall is located, but Daddy did. He knew about lots of hidden and interesting things that he'd stumbled upon while hunting, fishing, or just strolling about. We went to that waterfall a couple of times and after you climbed down a pretty steep limestone cliff, you took your life in your hands as you moved under the falls. One would take a pretty good pounding from the falling water.

The most famous hot spring in the area is the one that has been used as a spa for many years. In my time it was called Gregson Hot Springs. Long ago Indian tribes set up tepees in the trees near the twelve hot springs—"medicine waters"—they called them. Along came a pair of brothers, the Gregsons, and the bought the land from a squatter, paying him sixty dollars for the 320 acres.

First the brothers went into the dairy business; then, later on, they turned their attention to the twelve pools of hot mineral water. They built a two-story hotel that would house fifty to sixty guests. They built a plunge bath and five large bathing rooms. People came to "take the waters" for cures of all kinds of ailments. The two used a covered flume to transport hot and cold water to the bathhouses. Cold water was taken from a pure cold stream nearby and mixed with the too-hot-for-bathing mineral water. The spa also offered fishing and hunting for visitors interested in those pursuits.

The resort was a haven from the heat, dust, and miserable dirty work of the copper mines and the smelter where many of the local men worked. The spa wasn't just for the rich. Any wage group of people—day laborers, weary business people, invalids, as well as pleasure seekers—were welcome. Nothing was spared to make the stay of the sick and invalid as comfortable and beneficial as that of the tourist. Organizations and clubs held their annual picnics and parties at Gregson. They came by buggy, horseback, and train to enjoy the pleasures offered by the Gregson brothers.

Throughout the next half-century, Gregson suffered mismanagement, fires, and buildings and systems falling into disrepair. On the rare occasions when we went to the Springs to enjoy swimming in warm water, I was appalled by the disintegration of the interior of the pool buildings. Then, in 1972, the Fairmont Corporation of British Columbia, Canada, purchased Gregson Hot Springs. Fairmont has fabulous hotels and luxury venues all over the planet. Over the next few years the site was transformed.

The Fairmont Corporation built a new large and luxurious complex. The architect designed an indoor pool of eighty by 120 feet, and a larger outdoor pool with a smaller hot pool built right into the center of the larger pool. I once swam in the outdoor pool in the middle of the winter, crossing ice in bare feet to get to the warm water. While the pool water was pleasantly warm, the center pool was almost too hot. We sat in it, accumulating icicles in our hair while our bottoms cooked.

The Fairmont Corporation constructed lodging units; a lobby and shops; a convention center with two dining rooms, lounge, and coffee shop; a large modern kitchen; and also a cabaret on the second floor, which connected to the second floor west wing by a large bubble. You can stay inside the buildings at all times, unless you want to swim in the outdoor pool.

While the buildings certainly needed repair back there in my childhood, and while everything built by the Fairmont Corporation is beautiful and efficient and wonderful, I kind of miss the old Gregson Hot Springs and the wonder of all that hot water pouring out of the ground right at our feet. Montana—what an amazing place to grow up!

10

The Big Yellow Cat

I don't know where he came from, but I'll never forget him: a big yellow cat we named Tabby. He was the proud, fierce fighting kind of tomcat that spent the night out and dragged himself home all scratched and bleeding in the morning. He'd stay home for a few days while he healed, and then he'd be out again until the next time.

He came to us in the winter—and winters in Montana were bitter. Did that rate him a place to stay in our nice, cozy, warm house at night? Not on your life! Shortly after sundown, Mom would open the door and scoot him out. She never did let us keep a cat in the house at night. Litter boxes were not even considered. I'm not sure I ever saw a litter box in anyone's house in all those growing-up years in Montana.

I've been an animal lover from my earliest days, and I could hardly stand the thought of that big yellow cat out there in the bitter cold. When morning came, I went out as soon as possible to find him and see if he had survived the night. I really worried about him. One day we searched and searched. We finally found him sleeping off his night's binge curled way down in a hide that Dad had peeled off a deer and draped over some old tires to dry until he could sell it. That big orange cat was all curled up down in that fur and was just fine.

But that's not the reason we remember him more than the succession of cats that lived with us over the years. This one we remember because of his bravery and determination. One evening, this night warrior, as usual, set off on a nocturnal adventure. In the morning when we called, he was nowhere to be found. We searched the deer hide—no cat. We searched the sheds—no cat. We searched everywhere, but he could not be found. One cold day passed with no sign of him. We thought he probably had a girlfriend he did not want to leave, so we weren't too worried. Day two came, and when he had not put in an appearance, we began to wonder if he would come back. On day three we began to suspect he had been the victim of a bobcat down near the river, or perhaps he had fought some tomcat that was bigger, heavier, and meaner than he was. Or it could be that he had tangled with a car and lost.

After a while we gave up calling and watching for him. But like a funny little song that my kids used to like and sing, "The Cat Came Back," here came Tabby, dragging a trap with him. He had caught his front foot in one of those cruel spring-trap devices that grab on with a death grip and, because they are attached to a stake or a tree, the animal cannot get away even though it may still be alive. Such traps mean a slow, tortuous death to an animal. But Tabby, ingenious cat that he was, had chewed the whole trap free from its stake and dragged it home.

Dad forced open the jaws of that vicious trap and freed a very tired, thin, grateful cat. He had caught his foot at the toes, so he sat by the fire for several days with some bright pink toes that we thought might fall off from frostbite and lack of circulation. They didn't. He was just fine. Somehow, after that experience Tabby wasn't quite so ready to go out into the battle arena.

I don't remember what happened to that old tomcat. He was just one in a long progression of animals that came and went, but I will never forget him sitting by the big old kitchen range with three pink toes sticking out. He was a remarkable animal with a great sense of survival.

11

Camping Extraordinaire

Deer Lodge is located between two amazing and stunningly beautiful national parks. Yellowstone National Park is about 215 miles to the south, and Glacier National Park is about 209 miles to the north. Both routes to the parks pass through some of the most beautiful real estate in the world. There are amazing mountains reaching for the sky in the land of shining mountains. Crystal-clear streams flow through rich, lush meadows and plummet over cliffs. Fat Angus and Hereford cattle stand shoulder deep in the grass. Occasionally, there are glimpses of deer and elk hanging out at the edge of the timber, ready to flee into the deep woods if danger threatens. All this before you ever get to one of the parks. And both parks offer amazing camping opportunities in the middle of nature and all it has to offer.

Sometimes when I am buckling a child into a safety seat, I feel just a little sorry for him or her. That child will never know the freedom my kids experienced on long trips when I would fill up the space in front of the back seat with rolled-up sleeping bags, quilts, and pillows. My two could stretch out and sleep all they wanted. Sometimes I'd crawl back there and sleep too. And in my childhood, there was our homemade camper.

It was basically a wooden box Daddy made and bolted onto the back of a pickup truck. The box was cantilevered out over the rear wheels to make the "camper" a little wider. This arrangement formed a shelf on either side of the interior.

Daddy cut down an old mesh mattress spring so it fit across the gap from one side to the other. He put a mattress on the springs, and that was where we kids would ride. Underneath and lengthwise you could just fit another mattress. Mom and Dad slept down there when we were camping.

The camper had a canvas top that had been waterproofed. In the front of the camper, just to either side of the hood of the pickup cab, were two air vents we could open. It worked fine when we were moving, but when we stopped that box would heat up like an oven. The back door was hinged, and we could pull it up and put a stick under it to hold it in place. Sometimes the space under the propped-open door served as a place to get out of the rain.

The camper had one more feature: a pass-through to the cab of the pickup. Dad had cut a hole in the camper body that exactly matched the back window of the pickup. Then he had taken out the window of the pickup and fashioned a crude donut out of waterproofed canvas, which he had then attached to both the camper and to the pickup. The opening wasn't very large, but neither were we.

We would slide headfirst from the camper into the cab of the pickup, where we got to ride for a while. Most of the time, though, we just padded the opening with pillows and stuck our heads through so we could see what was going on up front. Sometimes the waterproofing in the window would fail a little, and we'd get a few drops of water dropping on our heads. It was in this setup that we travelled many miles, and it was in our homemade camper that we toured state and national parks and monuments.

* * *

In addition to beautiful meadows, streams, cattle, and brilliant blue skies, between Deer Lodge and Yellowstone Park are a couple of truly amazing and interesting state parks. One of these is the Madison Buffalo Jump. For 2,000 years, the Native Americans used the high limestone cliff at the edge of the broad Madison Valley as a buffalo jump.

Bison were essential to the survival of the Native American people. They used the skins for clothing and shelter and the meat for sustenance. Here at the Buffalo Jump, young men from local tribes would dress in buffalo, antelope, or wolf skins. One brave would move swiftly among the herds of bison that were so abundant in the area, give the signal, and the stampede was on. The buffalo would plunge over the cliff and to their deaths. Just in case any escaped, there were other young men with spears positioned on the sides and the bottom of the cliff to finish off the bison.

Standing at the top, one can almost hear hooves pounding toward the edge of the cliff. It's easy to imagine the whoops and cries of the hunters as they drove the frightened animals to their deaths through clouds of dust. Think of the joy in camp when the hunt was successful and there was meat to feast on and to dry for the long winter.

Just near the Buffalo Jump, at a place called Three Forks, are the headwaters of the Missouri River. Here the Jefferson, Madison, and Gallatin rivers merge to form the 2,300-mile Missouri River that winds its way eastward to join the mighty Mississippi. Meriwether Lewis, who traversed this way with William Clark, remarked on the way the country opens suddenly to extensive and beautiful plains and meadows that appear to be surrounded in every direction by distant, lofty mountains. The famous Sacajawea, the female Indian guide for the expedition, had been captured here as a child, carried away as a prisoner, and eventually returned as a member of the Corps of Discovery—a select group of volunteers who formed the nucleus of the Lewis and Clark expedition.

Also on the way to Yellowstone Park is the Lewis and Clark Caverns State Park. When I was a child, the Lewis and Clark Caverns were called Morrison Caves. Native Americans knew about the caves long before their discovery by explorers and settlers of the area. In 1805, Lewis and Clark camped within sight of the caverns but did not know they were there. Non-native (European) Americans "discovered" the caves in 1882 but told few people about them. Then, in 1892, local ranchers who were out hunting saw steam coming from the caverns. They still did not explore the caverns until six years later in 1898.

It wasn't until 1900 that Dan A. Morrison developed the caves for tours (thus the name "Morrison Caves"). Morrison called it "Limespur Cave." Finally, in 1908, the site was officially established as the "Lewis and Clark Cavern National Monument." It was a national monument until the site was transferred to the State of Montana. For many years after the name change, my folks still called it Morrison Caves.

I have been in a number of caverns around the country, including Carlsbad Caverns in New Mexico. Although other caves are larger and the tours longer, they have nothing to offer that is not found at Lewis and Clark State Park. There are gorgeous stalactite, stalagmite, and limestone columns in the cave. There's a "headache rock" where one has to crouch down to pass under, a fat man's misery where one must squeeze through a narrow limestone tube, and a formation that looks like strips of bacon with egg when a light is held behind them. The Lewis and Clark Caverns are a delightful side trip on the way to Yellowstone.

For many years while growing up, I heard stories about Yellowstone, where geysers—boiling hot water spewing out of crevices in the ground—and steam vents roared rotten-egg-smelling sulfur fumes. I heard about the thin crust of earth that separates mankind from the boiling cauldron just below the limestone-encrusted surface of soil. I was told about the constant buildup of limestone deposits at Mammoth Hot Springs, which caused it to look like a gigantic wedding cake. I was told it was possible to catch a trout at Yellowstone Lake and, without taking the fish off the hook and line, be able to boil it in a small geyser right in the lake. Oh, and one must not forget Old Faithful Geyser, which spewed steam and water into the air for a distance of 140 to 180 feet every sixty minutes to two hours.

The park has 10,000 thermal features, including geysers, boiling mud pots, steaming pools, and steaming fumaroles. There are three areas called "geyser basins" where most of the thermal activity takes place: the upper basin, the lower basin, and Norris Geyser Basin. The water play and the formations surrounding the openings in the earth have given the geysers some colorful names, including Castle Geyser, Sawmill Geyser, White Dome Geyser (with its twenty-foot dome), Plume Geyser, Lion Geyser, and Clepsydra Geyser, named for a Greek water clock. In 1959, when the 7.5 Hebgen Lake (now called Quake Lake) Earthquake happened, most of the pools and geysers in the park erupted simultaneously for a number of hours. But the first time I went to the park as a child the earthquake had not happened yet, and we could not have imagined the magnitude of such an event.

One summer, our double cousins and their parents—Mom's sister, Dad's brother—came to visit. We decided to go to Yellowstone Park and camp out. Grandma Cole wanted to go along. That was fine with all of us, and so our adventure began. My uncle Wayne had a rattle-trap of an old car that would heat (or vapor) lock. It would do this especially when we slowed down—such as to look at a bear begging on the roadway. The way to break a heat lock is to get out of the car, get some water, open the hood, and pour the water over the fuel pump.

I was riding in the back seat of his car with my cousins when, sure enough, we came around a corner and there stood a bear in the road begging for food. Of course, cars of onlookers were stopped ahead of us on the roadway. We had no choice but to stop, and when we slowed down, the car heat locked. We were trapped with a hungry bear standing on its hind legs, looking for the next treat. It gets worse. The window on the driver's side of the car wouldn't roll up. So, instead of trying to figure out how to rescue us, my crazy uncle decided to take a picture of the bear that now had its head in the window—just inches from us kids in the back seat. With a camera in his hands, Uncle Wayne backed as far across the front seat into the passenger area (practically into my aunt's lap) as he possibly could. Wild bear might look like sweet, tame cuddly things, but they are not. This was a wild animal intent on one thing—food—denied that one thing it could get very mean.

My dad, who was in the car ahead of us, saw what was happening. He came to the rescue by throwing some tasty food off the road, and the bear had to scramble down a small embankment to get it. Quickly, the two men raised the hood of the car and poured water over the fuel pump—probably from a canvas bag (called a "desert bag") that hung on the radiator cap at the front of the car. The car started, and the men slammed the hood and scurried back to their respective drivers' seats before the bear returned. We were soon on our way again, breathing a little easier.

After a while we arrived at our campsite and began setting up. Uncle Wayne had a big tent for his big family of seven, and we had the camper. There really wasn't any place for my grandmother to sleep except in the tent. That was just fine with her. She set up a narrow camp cot inside the tent somewhere near its flap door. After supper, we sat around the campfire telling stories and grew very sleepy from the high altitude, fresh air, and full tummies. Finally, the grown-ups decided it was time to bed down, and we went to our respective sleeping facilities.

While it was relatively quiet in the camper, there was a lot of commotion in the tent—a lot of laughing and carrying on. My mom just couldn't let a party happen without her. She had to know what was going on, so she crawled out of our homemade camper and padded over to the tent. Inside, the family was teasing Grandma Cole, saying, "Grandma, a big old bear is going to come up to the tent and come right in that flap where you are sleeping on your cot." At that moment my mother started fumbling with the tent flap, trying to get in. Well, Grandma screamed like a banshee. She was pretty sure a bear was about to attack her.

* * *

A number of years ago when my children were teens, we visited the Alps in Switzerland. I had heard about the Alps all my life, and while they were very green and beautiful—I loved looking way down in the valleys and listening for the sound of cowbells wafting up from what appeared to be miniature cows—I felt some disappointment. For a while I wondered if there was something wrong with me. Then I realized I had been totally spoiled by my visits to Glacier National Park. Glacier is stunningly beautiful, rugged, majestic, and filled with lakes, glaciers, and wildlife.

We went to Glacier National Park several times when I was a child, but the time I remember the most was when another family of cousins went with us. The Swants lived in Deer Lodge but had family in Walla Walla, Washington. They, like us, had a homemade camper on the back of a pickup truck in which they travelled back and forth to Washington State. Our parents decided that we would all go first to Glacier National Park and then on to Walla Walla. From there our family would proceed on to "the coast"—which is what we called the Puget Sound area of Washington State.

National Parks to this day are somewhat primitive places if you are camping out. Campsites are equipped with a table with benches and a fire ring where, weather and fire conditions permitting, you can have an open fire. While some campgrounds have flushing toilets, many have pit toilets—and though these toilets have been improved over the years, they are still pit toilets. If you have to take the trail there after dark, you need a pretty good flashlight, because you never know what you might encounter on the path.

You bring your own camp supplies and food. Perishable food needs to be kept in a cooler. Ours was a virtually indestructible dark-green metal Coleman cooler. All food needed to be locked in the car trunk or hung from the branch of a tree—somewhere away from sleeping campers. Putting food in your trunk did not insure safety. A hungry bear could tear open a trunk or a car door to get at food.

Wildlife was, and is, abundant in the national parks. That's part of the reason for going there. Back then, bears and porcupines were more abundant and active in the campsites than they are allowed to be today. Today, marauding bears that become too much of a nuisance are trapped and taken into the back country. But back then, you really never knew when you would meet one on the trail to the outhouse. Again and again my dad told us the bears really didn't want us; they wanted what we had to eat. Summer, when most campers are in the woods, is the same time period when bears are eating and packing on fat for their long winter hibernation, and they will eat almost anything.

One evening in Glacier Park at about supper time, Mom was standing at the campsite table peeling potatoes when a bear wandered up behind her on a path. We yelled, "Mom! Bear! Mom, watch out!" She replied, "uh-huh," and went on peeling potatoes. Dad finally got her attention and said, "Grace, there's a bear right behind you." This time she looked around and saw the bear not twenty feet from her. She moved this time, in a hurry, toward the truck where we were already in hiding. Dad, ever resourceful, took the pan of potato peels and tossed them into the bush. The bear diverted his attention to what had landed there and, after investigating the peelings, wandered off to harass other campers.

Later that evening, when we had bedded down in the camper and were drifting toward sleep, we heard a thump, thump, thump coming from under the truck. "It's a pack rat," Dad whispered. "Let's see if he will answer back." With that he thumped on the side of the pickup—thump, thump, thump. And, sure enough, that silly rat thumped back. It went on for several minutes until everyone tired of the game.

12

Making Stew on a Grander Scale

I don't remember what task had been assigned to us, but Dad had given us some job that caused us kids to be burning trash. We were probably in the middle of the house remodel and had been assigned the task of burning old boards ripped from the walls. Our house had plaster walls, and in tearing out the plaster to remodel, there was a lot of lath to burn. No one worried about air pollution in those days—and those of us who lived in Montana (Big Sky country) *truly* were not concerned. There was lots of room for smoke. We also didn't worry about polluting our streams or filling up dumps at that time. There were no landfills, and the river that ran through our town—the Clarks Fork River—ran orange with copper from the smelter upstream. It had a strange metallic odor.

My brothers and I used to go duck hunting up the river. As we wandered around in the damp and cold, we would often happen on an old cow head or bone, stripped of hide and meat and turquoise blue from being soaked with copper-saturated water. Looking back, all that pollution was a little more than scary. The river was not cleaned up until after I left home. Years later when I returned, I couldn't believe my eyes when I saw men fishing near the river bridge right in town. There had been no fish in our river. Nothing could live in that polluted water.

But back to our stew story. At our house, we had a fifty-gallon drum called "the burn barrel," and we burned everything flammable. Burning stuff reduced trips to the dump to a minimum. Given that the dumps were just that—places where garbage was dumped in decaying masses on the ground—burning stuff was probably a better option. It reduced the possibility of disease being carried from the dump by flies and vermin to the population.

In our family, we sorted burnable trash from cans and bottles (not many of those in a family that grows its own food). Dad contrived a unit for the kitchen that helped us sort refuse. It was something like a trash receptacle with a swinging door, similar to the ones that could be found on the street or in a park. It was made of particle board. Dad attached it to the kitchen wall with hinges on one side and a lever on the other side that fastened to a bolt on the wall. Inside this particle-board unit were two steel cans he fabricated just for this purpose—one to accept paper, the other garbage. Each rectangular can had a metal handle on the back that we could grab to carry the receptacle out to the garbage can in the alley or the burn barrel.

We didn't have a garbage disposal, so wet garbage—peelings, coffee grounds, stems, stalks, and egg shells (but no meat scraps, bones, or fat)—went into a bucket under the sink. When the bucket had enough sloppy garbage in it, one of us became the garbage disposal and had to carry it out to the compost pile to dump. We composted just about everything that was biodegradable long before it was fashionable to have a compost pile.

Our compost pit was rather an informal business. Dad would dig a hole one or two feet deep, and we would throw leaves, garden refuse, and kitchen waste into it. After a while a mound would build up. Periodically Dad would throw some dirt or manure over the decaying vegetation to hurry the decomposing process. He also turned the compost fairly often with a spade fork or a pitchfork to aerate it. By the following spring, the rich composted material was ready and he could add it to the garden.

On this particular late-fall morning, we kids were burning a pile of trash too big for the burn barrel in an area not far from the compost pit. On the top of the compost pit were some old vegetables we had gleaned at the end of the harvest and thrown there because they were inferior. The three of us decided it would be fun to create a giant stew. We found a five-gallon bucket and filled it half full with water. We put our "cooking pot" on the fire and then started throwing in all the old vegetables we could find. There were onions, carrots, cabbage leaves, and who knows what else. We didn't peel or trim them. We just threw them in dirt and all.

Before long, as we fed trash into the fire, that five-gallon kettle of stew started boiling. Then, for good measure, we added the head of a deer that had been left after hunting. It had been more or less frozen, so it was still in pretty good condition. Of course, we had no intention of eating the stew, but man it smelled good! We probably had half the neighborhood salivating. At the end of our task, we took a two-by-four and tipped over the bucket, dumping our lovely stew into the smoldering embers of the fire and creating a giant cloud of steam. That was great fun too!

13

The Williamsburg of the West

The Montana I grew up in was a relatively stable and peaceful place. But the history of Montana is loaded with tales of robbers, murderers, drunkards, extortionists, road agents, and all things unlawful. One of the most notable towns of the Gold Rush era was Virginia City.

Virginia City is a town frozen in time. When I was still in grammar school, our class took a field trip there. Even as a child I was amazed at the houses, stores, boardwalks, facades on the stores, and the tiny shops established to meet every need of the miners. Everything was weathered and ancient, but it was still all there. The town's Green Revival, Gothic Revival, and Italianate buildings are the original ones built by the first settlers of the community.

I remember sitting in the courtroom of the brick courthouse. It was the very place where some of the criminals now lying in Boot Hill Cemetery would have been tried—though those trials were such popular amusement that they were often held outside to accommodate the crowds that came.

Virginia City became the second territorial capital of Montana after the neighboring town of Bannack held the title for a short time. To this day, Virginia City is a living town of 150 year-round residents who host the West's best-preserved gold mining town from the 1860s. Visitors walk the same boardwalks that desperate robbers, murderers, and vigilantes once trod.

* * *

With the discovery of gold in the area—namely in Alder Gulch—the population of the placer gold mining communities of Nevada City, Bannack, and Virginia City exploded. During the 1860s these three towns were among nine boom towns along Alder Gulch that became home to 10,000 people.

Lawlessness became the way of life in the mining camps. Miners and those who followed them to the gold camps were largely uneducated people seeking an easy fortune. The miners in these camps routinely took large amounts of gold from the ground, and soon that gold flowed freely from their pockets to the town's saloons, brothels, and gaming institutions. Firearms were as an ordinary and accepted part of people's attire as their hats, and they didn't go anywhere without their guns. This mix was a recipe for problems, and because there was no law that followed the miners to the gold camps, lawlessness prevailed in Virginia City and all the towns along the gulch.

Robbery, murder, and mayhem continued until the 1860s, when a group of citizens formed a "vigilance committee" to bring some kind of law to the mining camps. The Montana Vigilantes, as they became known, have been both celebrated and condemned throughout history. In some cases they were as wild and lawless as the citizens of the camps, and the law became arbitrary. Vigilantes would capture an offender, and after a trial of sorts—no matter what proof was offered—the criminal was either hanged or set free, all in short order. If the criminal was well-liked in the community, he was usually judged not guilty. But for those who were not popular and were judged guilty, punishment was swift and brutal. In a two-year period from 1863 to 1865, it is estimated that the actions of vigilantes led to the hanging of between fifteen to thirty-five people. Many of the convictions were determined in secret trials.

One of the most notable of these clandestine trials was that of Henry Plummer. Plummer was born in Maine, but after his father died, he went west to California and the gold strikes there. California was good to him, and soon he owned a mine, a ranch, and a bakery. He even became the sheriff of a California town. Then he shot and killed a man. He was sentenced to ten years in San Quentin Prison, but after six months, Plummer was pardoned. After more trouble, he finally was told to leave the state. He then went to Washington Territory, where he got into another gunfight, which he won.

At this point, Plummer decided to return to his native Maine and started traveling east. He got as far as Fort Benton, Montana. Because there was no immediate way for him to continue on east, he accepted a position as the protector of a mission in southwest Montana. There he met and married his wife. Needing to provide a living for his wife, he decided to go to Bannack, where placer mining for gold was in full swing.

Once there, Plummer became the sheriff. It is believed that his office as sheriff was the perfect cover-up for him to operate an effective and deadly criminal ring. Some people believed it was Plummer who headed a gang that was responsible for nearly a hundred deaths. It is said that Plummer provided his henchmen with information on the movements of gold shipments and ensured they would not be captured when they robbed the gold.

Things went from bad to worse, and during the next six months, road agents terrorized the citizens of Bannack and Virginia City. Sheriff Plummer seemed unable, or perhaps unwilling, to stop them. It was then, in late December, the Montana Vigilantes consisting of nearly 2,000 members were organized. Two weeks after the formation of the committee, Henry Plummer and two of his lieutenants were arrested. While his lieutenants swore and resisted what was about to happen to them, Plummer reportedly wept and begged to be spared, to no avail. All three men were immediately and without further trial hanged on a Bannack gallows that Plummer himself had prepared. The vigilantes rode away, "leaving the corpses," as one contemporary wrote, "stiffening in the icy blast." Most of those hanged, Plummer included, ended up in Boot Hill Cemetery just outside Virginia City, having died with their "boots on."

We will never know whether Plummer was guilty of the crimes for which he was hung. What we do know is that the law of the Vigilantes was as brutal and sudden as that of the robbers, murderers, extortionists, and others they hung.

Virginia City began to decline after a few years when a new gold strike was found at Last Chance Gulch in the Helena area. Fickle miners chasing the elusive gold and the wealth it promised moved on and abandoned the town. A decade later, further harm was done when a railroad bypassed the town in favor of Helena. The territorial capital and government officials moved to Helena in 1875, and it became the capital of Montana. It remains so to this day.

The forests of Montana are full of rotting remnants of boom towns that miners established as they followed the almighty gold. A number of concerned citizens at first kept Virginia City from falling into ruin, but as time went on more funds were needed. It was a daunting task to find funding to restore the town and keep it operating as a tourist attraction. Then the National Trust for Historic Preservation became involved. They decided Virginia City was one of the nation's eleven most endangered historic places and realized it was a town that preserved the West as it was.

Several other attempts at finding funding failed. Then, during the 1950s, a magazine article named Virginia City "The Williamsburg of the West." That cranked the starter for the Historic Preservation society to approach the president of Colonial Williamsburg and the CEO of Biltmore House in Asheville to ask for help. The society asked them to send their top staff to Virginia City to give the team their best thinking on what should happen there. Also in attendance at the meeting were the president of the Montana Historical Society and the Director of Travel Montana. They heard experts from two of the finest museums in the nation share their ideas about transforming Virginia City into a world-class museum that told the story of how gold mining transformed the Western frontier.

In May 1997, the Montana Legislature passed a bill authorizing the state to purchase the historic buildings and artifacts of Virginia City and other nearby towns. The legislators noted they didn't pass the bill for tourism or economic development but to preserve Montana history.

Nevada City, just one and a half miles away, was included as part of the authorization. It has fourteen historic buildings original to the site plus a collection of more than 100 other historic buildings brought in from locations all over Montana. Fort Benton's Sullivan Saddlery, with its saddle-making equipment and a rocking chair where Charlie Russell, Montana's famous cowboy artist, spun yarns for listeners, are there. The Nevada City Music Hall features a world-class collection of music machines—the largest in the world—from player pianos to the world-renowned Gavioli Military Band Organ. The Star Bakery, an original 1863 Nevada City building, and the Nevada City Hotel offer bread and a place to stay.

May to September transforms Alder Gulch into a vacation destination. Horseback riding, a trip by stagecoach, and an expedition on the Alder Gulch Short Line Railroad across real gold country are journeys through transportation history. A 1941 fire truck—a concession to the automotive age—takes passengers on an entertaining tour of Virginia City's landmarks and lore. On special days, a restored 1910 Baldwin No. 12 steam locomotive pulls the railroad cars. Its presence is a strange reminder that the railroad furthered Virginia City's demise.

Along Wallace Street are shops of vintage clothing, Montana-made products, one-of-a-kind treasures, an old-fashioned candy store, and several museums. Along the unpaved back streets are modest cottages and lovely Victorian homes—some offering overnight accommodations in homes from another era.

One of the most memorable events I remember from my class trip to Virginia City was attending a melodrama performed at the Opera House. The Virginia City Players are

Montana's oldest professional theater troupe. In August of each year, the citizens hold the annual Grand Ball. It is a favorite topic all year long for participants, and they work at their dancing skills throughout the year. Then, when the weather warms, the participants promenade along Virginia City's wooden sidewalks in period finery.

All the towns along Alder Gulch went bust and became ghost towns. However, one "ghost town," Virginia City, lives on for all of us to enjoy, and there we can learn from the past.

14

Let's Go to the Dump!

Trips to the dump in the pickup with Dad were adventures. He usually went when we weren't around, because we always saw something we wanted to bring home. For many years there was no attendant at the dump and no fees for dumping. There were no bulldozers shoving piles of debris around, and there were no gigantic smashing, grinding machines to turn washing machines into compressed packages of steel in seconds. There was just blue sky and piles and piles of the off-scouring of our neighbors' possessions.

"Look, here's a good frying pan," we would say. "Why would someone throw out a perfectly good frying pan?" A treasure to be sure, whether we needed another frying pan or not. We just couldn't help but look at some piece of battered furniture and wonder if we'd ever seen it in a friend's house. The best times were when someone else was at the dump unloading. If we hung around long enough, we could see what they had thrown out.

When we were in high school, the dump provided another form of recreation: skunk hunting. Skunks overran the dump at night. They were there to feed on garbage and were fair game. There were plenty of skunks in our neck of the woods, and we knew no one would miss one or two. So bands of kids with twenty-two caliber rifles would go to the dump, usually at night, to shoot the skunks.

It sounds pretty primitive, and it was. But when you live in a little town of 4,000 people far from any other town, when you have no television because no one has ever heard of cable yet and the mountains surrounding the town effectively keep any TV signal away, and when you have more time on your hands than you know how to use, you invent things to do like hunting skunks in the dump at midnight. And no one thought anything about letting kids run around at night with 22s. Everybody had a rifle, and we were taught early in life to respect guns and what they could do. In all our growing-up years, we never knew anyone who was shot either intentionally or accidentally.

Every little community or group of farms across the countryside had its own dump, and Dad knew where they all were. It could be especially profitable for us to check out those sites, because people looking for treasures didn't often visit them. In those dumps one could find the kinds of things that are now being sold all over the country and on eBay as collectibles.

Especially useful to Dad was the railroad dump, where workers would throw out everything from batteries to nails. There were pieces of sheet metal, big pieces of plywood, wire, tools, and all kinds of stuff. When Dad was in the middle of a building project and needed something, instead of running down to the lumberyard or hardware store, he'd first go to the railroad dump to see what he could find. The railroad dump was as close, perhaps even closer than the lumber yard, so it wasn't a big deal for him to run by there. Dad would often stop by on his way home from work to check out the dump's offerings.

I don't know if it genetic or not, but Ray used to frequent the railroad dump too and bring home stacks of used batteries. He would wire up them up and run little lights from their power. The only problem was that he strung wires everywhere, and going into his room was like crawling into a spider's cave. There were strands of wire hanging from every imaginable and some unimaginable places.

The woods of Montana are full of old mining camps. You can identify some of the sites only by the piles of weathered lumber, silvered by the sun, wind, and snow for nearly a hundred years. That old lumber never saw a coat of paint and has now worn to a lovely rustic gray. In every mining camp, there was a dump. These days when you wander into a mining camp, you'll find holes everywhere, because people have dug for bottles. There aren't many left, but you might still find an old enamel bucket with holes in it, or a rusting Prince Albert tobacco can, or perhaps even a coffee can—the short one-pound size—with so much rust on it that you can only identify it by shape.

For me, the treasures in those old mining camp dumps were the bits and pieces of broken pottery scattered about. Here a two-inch square of flow-blue pottery, there a white ironstone piece with a lovely intricate pattern embossed on it. Tiny, dainty flower buds and leaves gave mute evidence to the women who had helped their men eke out an existence from their scratching in the ground as they searched for treasures of silver and gold.

First, there'd be a gold strike, like that of Alder Gulch, and then an influx of all kinds of humanity. In most cases, thousands of people would come in and put up log cabins or simple tar paper shacks rather than the lovely homes of Virginia City. Later, the gold would peter out, and the treasure hunters would be on to another place . . . another strike . . . another dream. When they left, they simply walked out and left much of their stuff behind—old iron beds, stoves, bottles, cans, and scraps of newspaper glued to the walls of their miserable huts.

Soon, what had been home to them became falling-down piles of rotting logs and silvered boards—silent evidence to broken dreams. Where once there had been vibrancy, their abodes quickly became the homes of mountain rats and all manner of hurrying, scurrying vermin. Once upon a time in these woods women cooked and served food on flow blue plates. Children played homemade games, and men worked small claims, ever hunting for the elusive gold.

So, whether we kids were making buckets of inedible stew, scouring a dump for treasures, or recycling in our own primitive way, we were never bored.

15

Bees and a Big White Goose

Almost every summer our family would make a trek from Montana to Washington State to visit our grandparents and the many other family members who were in that area. Most of them lived on farms or in small towns, and we found it a great adventure to visit them. If we went late in the summer, there were walls of blackberry vines and clusters of blackberry fruit begging to be picked. Getting to the berries was a challenge. We'd lean cardboard or boards against the tangle and then climb up on it. Our weight would carry the boards down to form more or less of a horizontal platform that we could use to stand on and pick berries. These were the big Himalayan blackberries, and you could fill a pail in half an hour. It was fun.

One uncle by marriage, Uncle John, was the manager of a large farm. His house was provided as part of his pay, and while it seemed large to me as a child, it was probably a rather simple white farmhouse. Behind the house were sheds and barns, and sweeping down and away from the house were the fields and corrals for milk cows. We kids pretty much had run of the place. Sometimes that was good, and sometimes not.

When Ray was about four years old, he was out investigating things around the farm and discovered an old trailer with fold-out doors on the top. It was probably a trailer for hauling farm machinery parts and tools out to the field to repair machinery. Whatever its reason for existence, Ray wanted to see what was in the trailer. So he crawled up on the tongue and lifted the lids. What none of us knew was that a swarm of bees was busy making a nest in the trailer. When Ray lifted the lid, a sentinel bee flew out and stung him. He reacted in a fairly normal manner—he dropped the lid. That did it! The whole swarm attacked him and began to sting him everywhere.

He was down on the ground, pawing and screaming, when someone ran to his rescue. When they brought him inside, Mom ran to the cupboard to get some baking soda to apply to the sting. Then she asked him, "Ray, where did you get stung?"

"All over! All over!" He screamed.

"Now, Ray," she said calmly, "it just feels like it. Where is the sting?"

"All over! All over!" he yelled.

Then she began to see that he was right. Bright red bumps were popping out all over his head. She ran back to the kitchen, dumped the entire box of baking soda in a bowl, ran some tap water into it, and rushed back to smear the mixture all over his head.

"I think you better call the doctor," Dad's sister, Aunt Bernice, warned.

So someone called the doctor. The doctor said we were to watch him carefully. If he showed any signs that were abnormal, or if he acted as though he were going into shock, they were to rush him to the doctor. To reduce the swelling, both Mom and Dad held ice cubes wrapped in washcloths on the most severe bumps. There were two problems with that. One was that the ice cubes would melt almost instantly, and the other was that while they were reducing the swelling in one spot, a sting would swell up in another spot. Mom and Dad sat with him all night long, watching him, praying, and applying ice cubes.

But before the long night's vigil began, Uncle John decided he'd get rid of the bees. Dad went to help him. They got their spraying equipment ready and waited until it was dark and the bees were all inside the trailer. Ray had reported seeing a "big bag of bees." A swarm. The two men carefully approached the trailer in the pitch dark. Dad was holding the light, while Uncle John had the sprayer. Carefully, ever so carefully, they lifted the lid. Immediately, John began to spray. A lone bee flew out, and Dad stepped backward as a normal response. When he did, he hit a big bull thistle, which stuck him right through his clothes. He ran.

"Hey, come back here with the light!" Uncle John yelled. He was in close proximity to the swarm, in the dark, with his hands full of spray equipment.

Sheepishly, Dad returned. When they came in, Uncle John went straight to Ray and told him he'd "got 'em." It was only a bit of comfort to the little boy who was suffering greatly.

* * *

A pasture was down the hill from the place where the trailer was parked, and in that pasture was a flock of geese. Big, white, noisy geese. We'd go down there to hang over the fences and watch the flock. They had been brought to the farm to weed strawberries. In theory, the geese were to eat the young grass growing up through the strawberry plants. I don't remember any great enthusiasm for the success of this idea, but here was this flock of geese as a reminder of the plan.

Uncle John looked at my brothers and said, "Tell you what. If you can catch one of those geese, you can have him." He was chuckling under his breath, because my brothers were just little guys and the geese were winged and not at all used to being chased by little boys. He knew they could never catch one. Well, those two set off to begin herding the geese into a corner of the fence. The geese kept squeezing out of formation and escaping—all but one. Glen and Ray continued to herd this one right into the corner, and then they closed in on him and caught him by the neck. That goose was so heavy they could scarcely pick him up, but they did. Uncle John just stood there with an I-don't-believe-it look on his face.

Dad shook his head. He was already wondering what we were going to do with a goose and how we were going to get it back to Montana. He encouraged the boys to let it go, but they would have none of it. There was nothing left for him to do but build a crate and put the goose in it for the long trip home. You haven't lived until you have traveled 600 miles in a pickup truck camper with a live goose.

We managed to get the goose home not only alive but also in good condition. We put him straight into the chicken house, where he began to terrorize the chickens. When one of us would fill the dishpan used for water for the chickens, he kept them far away. First, he drank and drank and drank. Then he got into the water and took a long bath. The poor chickens were standing there with their chicken tongues hanging out.

Then we discovered he was pretty tame and could be let out. We'd fill a depression in the lawn with water, and he would get in there and splash and splash. When someone came home, his loud honking let everyone know about the arrival. He would come to the back door to beg for scraps and would flap and honk right outside our eating area. It was sometimes hard to eat with that overfed goose standing at the door telling us he was starving to death.

Our chicken operation was rather simple. We got a bunch of baby chicks in March, fed them a feed that would put weight on them rapidly, and then, by fall, Dad would butcher them and put them in the freezer. So, at the end of the summer, we had to make a decision about the goose. We really didn't have any facility for keeping him through the winter. One day when we came home, we found that Mr. Goose had gone to goose heaven. He didn't reappear until much later at Christmas dinner. By that time, we'd more or less forgotten that he'd been a kind of pet.

16

Potato Picking

Our valley was noted for its production of seed potatoes. It seemed to be the perfect locale for producing disease-free seed. All up and down the valley, row upon row of green plants pushed their way out of the ground in spring and then grew lush and tall in the summer sun. About mid-summer they bloomed thickly with white blossoms, indicating tubers were forming below the soil. They grew rapidly in the long days of a northern clime where summer days began at half-past 4:00 and lasted until past 9:00. About mid-September while the days were still warm, the nights began to get chilly. And then one night there would be a killing frost that halted vine growth and matured the potatoes below the ground. It was time to pick them.

My first paying job was picking potatoes. I'd don my oldest, sturdiest clothing and go out to the fields. Dad never went, but Mom, my two brothers, and I would hit the fields so we could earn a little extra money to supplement our family's meager income. Mom always had a goal for her potato picking. One year she bought a lovely set of cream-ware Johnson Brothers pottery from England. She'd seen it in Sears Roebuck catalog and decided she wanted a good set of dishes for when company came over. Another year it was a set of kitchen chairs that we desperately needed. The chairs she bought were the good old chrome and vinyl kind that were popular in the late '40s and early '50s, and then went out of style completely until recently. They are now a popular item, and the original chairs are worth quite a bit. But we have only one chair left—the one Daddy sat on every morning at the kitchen counter.

So, on a crisp fall morning, we'd crawl into our clothing and drive out to the potato field. Once there, we'd see a piece of machinery known as a potato digger being pulled along the rows by a farmer on a tractor. The machine churned up the soil and left the potatoes lying smooth and golden on the top of the earth. I can still remember the feel and weight of those six-inch earth-dampened tubers—netted gems, they were.

At the end of every row there was a stack of wire buckets and a pile of gunny sacks. It was our job to fill those buckets with potatoes and then dump them into the sacks. We'd hold the wire buckets between our knees and tip them so we could dump the potatoes into the sack quickly. Holding the bucket in this way produced a nice set of matching bruises on the inside of our knees by the end of the day. It was pretty easy to empty the first bucket into the sack. We'd fit the sack under the lip of the bucket and tip the potatoes in. The hard part was lifting that second bucket, holding it, and fumbling open the top of the gunnysack without having it tip over or spill the potatoes that were already in it. Then we would have to dump the second bucket into the sack. It was hard, back-breaking work, but it was also very satisfying work because it was so elementary. We were taking food from the ground with our own hands.

The pay was ten cents a bucket or twenty cents a sack. As we picked, we lined up the sacks along the rows like sentries standing guard. Because there were lots of potatoes, there were lots of sacks, and for us the pay was just great. As kids we weren't terribly concerned about how much we made. A little was good. I can't imagine how many potatoes mother picked to earn enough for those dishes. We'd pick with her on Saturday, but she'd pick all through the week while we were in school. Potato harvest only lasted a couple of weeks, so when it was time to pick, that's what we did. The crop wouldn't wait for us to feel like picking, and neither would the farmers who were dependent on this income to keep their farms operating.

We usually worked at the farm nearest town, but sometimes we worked at other places. There was no bulletin board in town that notified us of which field was being picked. There was no Internet to tell us, and there was not even an announcement on the radio. We didn't even have a local radio station. There was just this incredible communication system. In our valley word traveled quickly. Perhaps it wasn't a grapevine that news traveled on, but a potato vine. Everyone seemed to know just about everything going on in the county almost as it was happening. Good news . . . bad news . . . it all raced up and down the communication highway of the Deer Lodge Valley. We usually knew within a few hours who had been in an accident, who had won a prize, when the next community picnic was scheduled, and who was digging potatoes and looking for workers. If I sat down to figure out how this communication system worked, I couldn't tell you. Everybody just knew, if they cared to know.

Once we'd completed a row of picking and our sacks were standing all along it, a farmhand would drive a big flatbed farm truck down the row and other field hands would lift the sacks onto the truck. They tabulated the sacks on a chart alongside our names. We also kept track of how many sacks we'd filled.

We'd work half a day, stopping occasionally throughout the morning to get a big drink of water from a brown thermos jug that we'd brought from home. Then we'd start again and keep picking until noon. A few times we were invited into the farmhouse to eat with the field hands and family. Usually, however, we would just wipe as much dirt as possible off our hands and sit down at the end of the row in some soft grass to eat our sandwiches, apples, and maybe a cookie. We'd rest a little, have another big drink of water, and afterward get back to work. By the end of the day we were filthy, but filthy with good earth dirt and not the dirt of cities. We smelled of the soil and not of carbon monoxide from the fumes of cars.

By the end of the day, we kids were usually a lot dirtier than Mom. Of course, we'd get tired and lay or sit on the soft ground, soaking up the warmth of the soil beneath us and the rays of the September sun. We'd go get our pay and, for a while, we'd feel like the richest people on earth. We'd plot and plan how we were going to spend our hoard. It's funny now, from this perspective on life, that I can't remember one thing I ever bought, but I vividly remember the experience of earning the money. Perhaps there is a great truth here: the experiences we have on our way to achievement are far more valuable to us in the long run than the achievement itself.

If you have never really gotten dirty at hard work, then you've probably never experienced the true pleasure of a hot bath. If your muscles have never screamed from exertion, then you probably don't understand the healing nature of soaking in a tub. When we came in from the potato fields, we'd go one after another to the tub to scrub off the evidence of our labor. Of course, with only one bathroom and several people needing to use it, soaking was out, except for the last person. Hmmm. Maybe that's why Mom went last. I always thought she was just being generous in letting us go first.

Some time during potato picking season, we had to get our own potatoes out of the ground and into storage for the winter. Of course, there was no pay for picking potatoes at home. But there were lessons to be learned whether we were picking for pay or picking for the family's well being. Potato picking taught us early in life the satisfaction of a job well done and the sense of accomplishment we could derive from even the simplest of tasks. We learned how sweet and restorative sleep could be after a day of hard, backbreaking work. We learned the comfort of getting clean after being so dirty. We learned the pleasure of provision at its most elementary level by taking real food from the soil as we did when picking potatoes.

We always said Dad was a "meat and potatoes" man. Maybe the reason for this was that these were the things he could provide for us, much in the same way the ancient hunters and gatherers and the early farmers provided for their families since the dawn of time. Dad took game from the wilds, berries from the hills, and vegetables from his garden, and we never went without any good thing.

17

One Hundred Years and Counting

Deer Lodge is the second oldest town in Montana. It was originally called LaBarge City, then Spanish Fork, Cottonwood, Deer Lodge City, and finally just Deer Lodge. It is a small town, but those who think small towns are boring have obviously never lived in one. There is an inner life in small towns that is vibrant and dynamic. Sure, you don't have big productions by professional companies (unless you're talking rodeos). No, you don't have major league sporting events. But you do have neighbors getting together to put on plays, musical events, their own sporting events, and home-style rodeos for one another. Such an event happened when I was in high school. It was the centennial celebration of the discovery of gold in Montana.

I remember that in honor of the occasion, stores in town faced all their buildings with slab lumber. You know, the kind that still has the bark attached. Many of the shops also constructed vintage porches and covered walkways of wood for the occasion. It truly gave the town the feel of the Old West a hundred years earlier, complete with cowboys and miners and lumbermen—and, yes, gold miners.

The town folks decided to have a pageant depicting the discovery of gold in the county. All the actors were local people. The rodeo grounds were transformed into a huge stage. We all sat in the grandstand and watched the show depicting the history of Deer Lodge. It went something like this.

Gold was first discovered in Gold Creek, Montana. In 1852, a trapper named Francois Finlay, who was also known as Benetsee, found the first recorded gold in Montana in a creek he named Benetsee Creek. Six years later, in 1858, prospecting brothers James and Granville Stuart and Reese Anderson rediscovered gold in the creek, but this time in an amount significant enough to warrant mining it. The three men had no tools to begin excavating. They had no provisions either, except the game they killed. To mine their rich strike they had to have tools and provisions, so they killed and dried enough meat to eat to get them to Fort Bridger on the Overland Trail, where they could buy the necessary supplies for a longer stay in Deer Lodge Valley. The party left for Fort Bridger on June 16, 1858.

The Stuarts did not return until two years later in 1860. They came back with the proper equipment and began mining. While it wasn't terribly original, they named the creek where they dug "Gold Creek," for obvious reasons. The discovery of gold helped open up Western Montana to settlers.

The Native Americans used the wide, flat sixty-mile long Deer Lodge Valley as a path for their hunting journeys. They called the Blackfoot River, located in the county, the Cokallanishkit, or "The River of the Road to the Buffalo." Later on, gold was discovered in several other locations around the area, including Pioneer City, Ophir, Blackfoot City, Bear Gulch, and Elk Gulch. Deer Lodge then became known as the "Little Town on the way to Bear," a roaring mining camp in Bear Gulch. The old mining camp of Pioneer City on Gold Creek is said to have yielded more than $20 million in gold during the 1860s. Later on, after the Caucasians abandoned the camp, the Chinese moved in and worked the ground. At one time there were more than a hundred Chinese in Pioneer City.

John Francis ("Johnny") Grant, a son of Captain Richard Grant of the Hudson's Bay Company, was probably the first permanent settler in Powell County. He built two log cabins and corrals at the mouth of the Cokallanishkit in November

1859. Grant had merchandise for sale and traded with the Indians. He did a thriving business. In another venture, he and others purchased worn-out cattle from emigrants crossing the continent on the Overland Trail. The valley had excellent pasture for these cattle, and the stock grew fat. Herders drove the cattle down the trail for resale. As you can imagine, the profits were large. Soon, several other men built cabins close to Johnny Grant's house, and the settlement became known as Grantsville.

In the winter of 1860, other settlements began to be developed in the valley. Tom Lavatta had a house on Cottonwood Creek about a mile above Deer Lodge. Joe Hill had a cabin nearby, and so did several Mexicans. For a time, that gave the community the name Spanish Fork. The Stuarts and others were still digging at Gold Creek, which was known as American Fork. The Stuarts also planted grain crops and became the first farmers in the valley.

In the summer of 1863, Johnny Grant moved from the Little Blackfoot to what is now Kohrs Ranch just north of Deer Lodge. There he built the first pretentious house in Montana, which is still part of the ranch. It was two stories high and had twenty-four glass windows and green shutters. Johnny was one of the wealthiest citizens of the territory. Later on, in 1868, he sold his cattle to Conrad Kohrs and moved his family to a location near Winnipeg, Canada. This herd of cattle was the beginning of one of the best-known and largest stock outfits of Montana, the Kohrs Cattle Company.

That's a bit of the history of the town. So, during that centennial summer of 1952, we ladies all donned our long dresses and shawls and bonnets to play the parts of our female ancestors of the city. The men donned chaps, cowboy hats, grew beards (my dad's beard was red while his hair was black, which we thought was very funny), and they too played the part of the early settlers of our valley.

Every town in the nation has a story, a beginning, and a rich history. Perhaps not all towns get their start with a gold discovery like ours, but they do have a history. Getting to know and celebrate that history, and what it has meant to the formation of the life you have in the place you live, is a worthy pursuit that enriches the lives of those who seek it.

18

Working in Montana

A lot of the work we did while growing up in Montana was simple, manual labor. Besides picking potatoes, the boys worked on ranches and I babysat. When they were a little older, they both fought fires. One year, Ray had a job on a road crew that was repaving a stretch of highway in the valley. Glen did some retail work, and Ray and I both taught swimming lessons a summer or two. That's about all there was for kids to do to earn a little extra money.

My brothers' main job on the ranches was haying. They both spent many summers on farms around our area lifting bales onto wagons and then lifting them off the wagons into barns. It was back-breaking work, but it also really packed muscles on them. They learned about overshot hay stackers and beaver slides that were used in constructing haystacks in our valley. They learned very quickly to stay out of the way of an overshot or get knocked off the haystack. They learned just how to use a beaver slide to build a haystack that wouldn't fall down midway through the winter.

* * *

Both of my brothers worked on the Kohrs Ranch, which is located at the north end of Deer Lodge. It is now a historical site that attracts thousands of visitors each year. At the time we were growing up, Conrad Warren managed it. His wife, Nellie, was Conrad Kohrs's granddaughter. Grandfather

Kohrs had bought the ranch from Johnny Grant. By the turn of the twentieth century, Kohrs and his half-brother, John Bielenberg, had turned Johnny's original herd into one of the largest cattle ranches in the nation, grazing their cattle on ten million acres in four states and two Canadian provinces. When we were children, the Kohrs Ranch was still one of the largest ranches in the valley. It was a fascinating place.

One of Glen's best friends was Conrad's son, and the two boys had many adventures in the old buildings at the ranch. At that time the main buildings included a simple white house where the Warrens lived, the old original ranch house built by Johnny Grant, bunkhouses for ranch hands, a blacksmith shop, stables, and miscellaneous farm buildings. Conrad Warren built a huge Quonset-styled barn near the family home that was surrounded by corrals and the machinery necessary for operating a large ranch operation.

One summer Mother had been very ill. Glen was working at the Kohrs Ranch, and we decided to let Mom get as much rest as possible. Because Glen had to be in the fields early, he would get up first, make the coffee, and bring me a cup so I could wake up while drinking it. I'd help him pack a lunch and then drive him to work. It was a special and pleasant time for the two of us and one that I remember fondly.

It was still fairly early one day when we got a call to come get Glen. He had fallen off the tractor between it and the hay wagon, and the hay wagon had run over him. It's unbelievable, but there were no injuries except for some pretty serious bruises and sore muscles. It was only one of several miracles Glen encountered growing up.

*　*　*

Ray worked for a short time at a greenhouse, and one of the tasks he was given to do was clean out a flue. I will never forget what he looked like when he came in from work. He was coal black—every inch of him. It took two or three baths to get the soot off him, and for a while the grime stayed around his fingernails and in the creases of his skin.

Another time when he was working for the road crew, he came in, sat down at the dinner table with us, and said, "One of the guys had an accident today." We expressed our concern and asked what happened. He said, "He ran over a cat with the steam roller." Believe me, with our love of animals that really got us moaning. Finally, one of us asked the right question: "What happened?" With a deadpan face, Ray said, "He just picked it up and stood there with a long puss." Laughter broke out, and we just howled with delight at his joke on us.

* * *

As for the work the grownups did, there was the smelter where Dad and Uncle Marvin worked for years and years. There was also mining at underground mines in the Butte area. During our growing-up years, the Berkley Pit was opened in the center of the city of Butte, just thirty-five miles from Deer Lodge.

The Berkeley Pit was an open-pit copper mine. After the first shovel was put in the ground, the pit began to grow. Humungous trucks crawled down roads into the pit, where they were loaded with as much copper ore as they could carry. Then they began the long, grinding trek back to the top, where the ore was dumped onto a conveyor belt and taken away for refining. Deeper and wider the pit grew. We kids were fascinated by the eventual mile-long by half-a-mile wide pit that was almost 1,800 feet deep. It would take our breath away to peer over the edge of that cavernous hole. Trucks with tires taller than two men, one standing on the shoulders of the other, looked like small Tonka toys when at the bottom of the pit.

The pit was started in 1955 and ceased operation in 1982. By then nearly one and a half billion tons of material had been removed, including more than 290 million tons of copper ore. The Berkeley Pit enabled Butte to lay claim to the title "the Richest Hill on Earth."

The pit, operated first by Anaconda Copper and then by ARCO, is an environmental nightmare. Once ARCO abandoned it and stopped pumping out ground water, the pit began to fill with water from surrounding aquifers. The water level began to rise at the rate of one foot a month to a depth of 900 feet. The water isn't so much a problem as what's in it. It is highly acidic and laden with heavy metals and dangerous chemicals that leach from the rock. These include arsenic, cadmium, zinc, and sulfuric acid. The water is so acidic that it allows pyrite and sulfide minerals in the ore and wall rocks to decay, which releases even more acid. There are so many dissolved minerals that some have been mined directly from the water.

It's a toxic soup, for sure. No fish live there, and no plants line the shores. There aren't even any insects buzzing about. In 1995, a flock of migrating snow geese stopped at the massive pond for a rest, and at least 342 of them died there. Authorities now use firecrackers and loudspeakers to scare away migrating waterfowl, but there have been a few smaller die-offs nonetheless.

While the pit was in operation, the water pumps kept the nearby mine shafts free of water. However, after the pit was abandoned and the pumping stopped, water ran into the mines. There is more bad news. The water level in the pit will eventually reach the natural water table. The time when it will happen is estimated to be about 2020. At that point, the pit water will reverse flow back into surrounding groundwater, polluting Silver Bow Creek—the headwaters of the Clark Fork River that flows through the middle of Deer Lodge and some of the most beautiful farmland in the nation.

That danger has earned the area the dubious distinction of being one of the EPA's largest superfund sites. Normally, technicians treat the water by adding lime to it to reduce the acidity and remove much of the metal. However, the Berkeley Pit is so huge and so saturated with undesirable minerals that this process would produce tons of toxic sludge every day. Other methods are safer but prohibitively expensive. Currently, the EPA's plan is to focus on containment.

In the meantime, if you are interested, there is a museum and a visitor's viewing platform where you can stand and gaze into the deep turquoise waters of the Berkeley Pit. If you have Google Earth, take a look at it. It's easy to see.

* * *

Of course, the biggest industry in the Deer Lodge Valley is still ranching. Fat, sleek Hereford cattle feed in the lush meadowland grass, chewing away and packing on pounds. There are also Black Angus and blond-colored cows (almost with white coats) called Charolais—a beef breed that originated in France. They are often crossed with Angus or Hereford. Much of the valley's life was wrapped tightly around the cattle industry. There were cattle sales and shows, rodeos and roundups, cattle drives and fencing, horses and ropes, and so much more that was necessary in raising beef cattle.

The other major industry in our area was logging and lumber. I don't know a lot about the lumber industry. What I knew was how a hillside looked after it had been clear-cut. To me it looked like a gigantic scar on the side of the mountain. I was told that clear-cutting, rather than trying to thin the forest by selective cutting, was the best way to go. I knew that once the canopy of trees was removed, a different kind of vegetation grew in those areas. When stripped of tall trees, the slashes were optimum places to find the succulent Montana huckleberry with its un-imitable flavor. There is nothing in the world more tasty than warm huckleberry pie with ice cream.

Because trees are a renewable resource, after clear-cutting the foresters would replant seedlings, and in a few years you could find a miniature forest growing and beginning to crowd out the huckleberries.

* * *

There were other jobs in Montana, just as there are anywhere. My mother was an award-winning accountant for the Ford Motor Company. Once in a while she would even sell a car. She worked in that job for many years, and at the end of her career she became the county treasurer for a few years. There were also teachers and salespeople, religious workers and shop keepers. All were needed, and all were necessary to the life of the little town.

* * *

Around home our work consisted of cleaning, feeding animals, weeding, doing the dishes after the evening meal, bringing in the laundry from the clothesline, and folding it. I ironed about a million shirts for the men in our family during my growing-up years. Ironing Daddy's blue chambray work shirts was a lot like ironing a tent. To make an unbearable task bearable, I listened to the Metropolitan Opera on the radio. It's true. I was fascinated by the stories, the voices, the orchestras, and the commentaries—all of it.

We were taught as children that work was good and should be embraced rather than avoided. We were also taught that "any job worth doing is worth doing well." And, so that we did not forget, sometimes we had to do the job again and again until we got it right. It must have worked, as all three of us tend toward being workaholics. We all still really enjoy doing a job well.

19

The Garden

It seems rather bland to say "the garden," but that's what we always called it. "Where's Dad?" we'd ask, and the answer from mid-April to mid-September was often, "He's in the garden." The garden did not include flower gardens or even a greenhouse. It consisted of beautiful weed-free straight rows of vegetables, raspberries, strawberries, corn, cabbage, kohlrabi, rutabagas, parsnips, carrots, and lettuce of all varieties.

The "big garden on Kentucky Street," as it was known, didn't just magically appear. It began months before any seed was put in the ground. Every year on Dad's birthday, March 12, he would get out the little plastic cups used for serving communion in his church. He picked them up after the service, took them home, washed them, and saved them until it was time to plant tomatoes.

Dad had big hands, which sometimes made him clumsy when handling small objects. He devised a neat process for planting small seeds in little pots with those big hands. First, he'd fill the communion cups with finely sifted soil. Then he'd touch the end of a wooden match to water, and then touch the seed with the end of the match. The seed would adhere to the wet match. He could then transfer the seed to the pot and push it into the soil to the exact depth he wished. He would place the communion cups in a tray on a tabletop near the sunniest window in the house. Day after day he'd watch and wait. A cousin who visited him during tomato seeding time said he checked them daily, babied them, and almost breathed life into the little seedlings.

Often, the seeds were from his prize tomatoes of the year before. The process of saving the seeds was as simple as biting a hole in the best tomato of the year, sucking out the seeds, and spitting them onto a paper towel. He'd pat them and spread them out to dry in the sunny window of his shop.

As soon as the seeds were up and growing, he transferred the tiny plants to the bottom halves of milk and juice cartons that he had saved and cut down for this purpose. He'd fill them with his own choice blend of potting soil. Montana's soil is very alkaline, so Dad often fed his baby tomato plants skim milk to provide the acid they needed. The acid produced by the souring milk made up the difference in pH balance. Perhaps it was a myth, or perhaps there were soil additives he could have used that would have achieved the same results, but his method was simple and inexpensive, and he thought it worked okay. Something did. Year after year he'd turn a handful of seeds into a couple hundred pounds of tomatoes. All these he grew in the greenhouse, where the plants were protected from the vagaries of Montana's "summer" weather.

* * *

Dad was a master gardener and had a great love for the soil and what it could produce. It began, he contended, with the quality of the soil. He built up the soil and built up the soil and built up the soil. When Dad put in his garden on Kentucky Street, he first picked up the rocks left by the glacial age. The valley where Deer Lodge is located is full of glacial till. There are round rocks and boulders everywhere, and the corner where the garden was located was no exception. Then Dad had the plot plowed, which completed the easy part of the job.

The next process was picking up more rock that had been turned up, and then screening every bit of the remaining dirt to remove sticks, stones, weeds, tree roots, and anything else too large to pass through the screen. Over the years, he used many processes to screen dirt. Once he used an old, old bedspring that didn't really have springs, but a kind of mesh webbing. (I think it might have been the same one we used in the camper.) He propped the "springs" at a forty-five-degree angle and threw shovels full of dirt against it. It worked great, except that he had to pull bits of sticks, grass, and small rocks out of that webbing, which was a nuisance.

His consistently favorite device was a four-legged contraption of his own design. It was basically a table with a screen bottom. The screen was recessed about four inches from the top to form a lip that held the unsifted dirt. He would throw shovels full of dirt on the top until the screen was pretty full. Then he would shake the whole sifter until all the dirt had fallen through the quarter-inch mesh and all that was left on the top were the stones and sticks. He'd dump the debris into a wheelbarrow to be hauled to a rock pile.

When the pile of dirt below the table grew almost to the bottom of the screen, he'd move the apparatus to a new location and continue the process. By the end of the day, the garden patch looked as if some giant mole had spent a very busy night pushing up soil. We kids understood this process well, because we did not escape helping by shaking that screen and moving that wheelbarrow full of sticks and rocks to a rock pile. Eventually, the rock pile had to be transported to the local dump.

After the screened soil was spread out, Dad would begin the process of adding the stuff that really made the garden grow. Mom used to have a saying: "It's not the salad dressing you put on the lettuce that makes it good; it's the manure." While the concept seems rather crude, it bears a lot of truth. Dad would come home in the pickup from some of his wanderings with a twinkle in his eye. "I found a place where there's a lot of old rotted horse manure," he'd say. "Boy, that would really make the vegetables grow!" Or he'd say, "You know those old sheep sheds up on Dempsey Creek? Well, there's a lot of old sheep manure there. I'm gonna ask the ranch owner if I can get some for the garden." He'd get a shovel, and off he'd go to get his treasure. It wasn't as bad as it sounds. Thoroughly rotted manure doesn't have much of a manure odor. It smells more like earth with a slightly pungent smell. Shoveling it onto a garden isn't the awful task one might think.

After Dad spread the manure, he had to work it into the soil. This required more shoveling and soil turning. Dad would also add field-grade fertilizer to the soil, which he could buy in fifty-pound sacks at the grain elevator. It was inexpensive when purchased that way. He felt that if it made crops grow in the fields, it would certainly make crops grow in a garden—and it did. He put it on the garden and on the lush, thick lawns all around the house.

But the real treasure for the gardens, especially the flower gardens, was black dirt. He probably knew every depository of black dirt in the county. We'd be out in the woods, and he'd say, "Just look at this." Then he'd push back some leaves, shove a spade down into the soil, and turn over the blackest soil we'd ever seen. "I'm coming back next week to get some for the garden," he would say, and he would.

That "black gumbo," as he called it, would turn fairly quickly into something that looked like lumps of coal (and be just about as hard as coal) unless he mixed it with soil, manure, and his other magic ingredient: rotted sawdust. He knew where old sawmills had been and where the sawdust had lain undisturbed for years and years, and he'd add that to the soil mix. Sometimes he'd think the sawdust was adequately rotted, but it wasn't. Then we'd hear him lament, "I think I burned the garden with that sawdust. It must not have been rotted enough." He would actually grieve because he had injured his plants. But nature has a way of righting itself, and the next year after the "too green" sawdust application, he usually had bumper crops.

* * *

When at long last the soil had been prepared and leveled, and the ground temperature was just right (usually in mid-

May), Dad would plant. First he'd set the stakes at the ends of the rows, then string lines between the stakes to make sure his furrows for seeds were straight, and then begin the trenching for seeds. He knew just how deep to make the trench for each type of seed, and he had a neat way of sowing seeds that were tiny—like carrot and lettuce seeds.

He mixed them thoroughly with fine sand and laid that mixture down in the trenches. This spread the seeds out and showed where they had been laid down. Then he'd get down on his knees and crawl along the rows sowing tiny seeds, trying not to put more in than were needed. He was a great believer in thinning vegetables severely. After a row had been planted, he'd crawl back along it and gently cover the seeds, tamping the earth firmly with a flat board.

Dad was a meat and potatoes man, and for him that meant growing his own potatoes. So after the seeds were planted, he'd go get his seed potatoes. Sometimes he saved them from the year before, but sometimes he'd have to go to the local feed store or the hardware store for new seed. I think his favorite potatoes were Netted Gems, but sometimes he tried Irish Rose. Usually he grew a few red potatoes to eat with peas, since peas and the red potatoes came on about the same time. Occasionally he'd buy his seed potatoes from a local potato farmer. He *never* used potatoes from the grocery store for seed.

Dad would get a stool to sit on and a galvanized bucket with a bail. He'd sharpen a knife with a whetstone that was so worn it was concave in shape. He'd sit down to cut the potato into pieces, with each piece having two or three eyes, since that's where the roots form. He'd bend over, pick up the potato, examine it, and then cut, cut, cut, plunk, plunk, plunk, into the bucket it went. Then he'd dig holes about six-inches deep in a straight line and drop a couple of pieces of potato into each hole. The last step was to cover the holes.

Once the seeds and potatoes were in the ground, the real challenge began. If it stayed warm enough to germinate the seed, he considered it a good beginning. Once the seedlings were up, there was often danger of frost occurring late into mid June, or early frost in the fall occurring as early as the end of August. Sometimes the seedlings came up and would not grow because of cold, rainy weather all through May and June. He used to say, "I don't know why I bother with a garden." But he always did.

In a fairly normal year, the challenge was to keep the soil moist enough for the seeds to germinate. This was where Dad displayed his real love of gardening. He would get that stool, go sit in the garden with a hand sprinkler turned to a fine spray, and gently water the soil. He held the spray in one place just until a little water pooled on the surface of the soil, and then he moved the spray to a new location. Over and over, back and forth, he'd move the nozzle until the entire garden was damp to the correct depth. In later years, he had a stool in each garden plot so he could sit wherever he happened to be. He nailed a board to the bottom of the legs to form a platform so the stool would not sink into the soil when he put his weight on it. As kids we had a lot of tasks to do, but I don't remember many of them being associated with the garden. That was Dad's domain—his pride and joy. His creative effort.

* * *

It wasn't until after we'd left home that Dad decided to go for growing tomatoes big time. Having gardened in Montana for many years, he knew it would be impossible to grow tomatoes outside. The growing season is simply too short. So he excavated the hillside above the big garden and set a greenhouse into the hillside.

Inside the ten-foot by fifteen-foot building, he built a raised bed all the way around using railroad ties he probably picked up from some tie replacement effort and got for free. He filled this bed with his choicest potting soil. About mid-May, he carried the seedlings now in milk cartons out to the greenhouse and set them into the raised beds. He manufactured a support system from four-inch steel concrete reinforcing grid material, wrapped it into a cylinder, and placed it over the seedlings. The four-inch grid made it possible for him to get his big hands inside to care for the young plants, and the steel was strong enough to support the bumper crops of tomatoes he consistently grew year after year.

Dad attached all these grids together with wires and twine. When he came into the greenhouse in early summer, he would grab the nearest steel cage and shake it. This caused all the cages to vibrate at the same time. "There are no insects in the greenhouse to pollinate the blossoms," he explained to wondering onlookers. "When I shake it like that, it does the job."

Every morning when the sun started to warm things up, he'd go out and open the greenhouse door. And every evening when it started to cool off, he'd walk down to close the door. If frost threatened, he'd sometimes put a small heater in the closed greenhouse. He also had some old rugs and canvases he used to pull over the greenhouse to protect the young plants.

Usually, when we arrived home for a visit in the summer, we first got a hug and then had to go to the greenhouse to see how the "tomatees" were doing. As we walked into the tiny greenhouse where one occupant could not pass another in the narrow aisle, we would instantly get a whiff of growing things: moist soil, tomato vines, and sometimes a geranium plant that was allowed inside to get a good start on summer (and, because it was doing so well, never made it back outdoors).

Dad would then explain how he cut off the water suckers along the tomato vines so all the strength went to the tomatoes and not into growing vines. He'd show us how he cut back the plants to a certain height instead of just letting them roam all over the greenhouse. He'd show us the resulting sturdy stalks looking like small trees, and he'd proudly show us the burgeoning green tomatoes forming all over each plant. "I think we're gonna have a couple hundred pounds this year," he'd say.

* * *

Dad also had a cold frame, which is just a box set into the ground with a translucent lid on it. At first he used it to start cabbage, but later on he grew cucumbers in it. He hated cucumbers. The only reason he grew them was to have pickles—which he loved. A cold frame is just a starter box, and while he let the cucumbers stay in it the whole season, after the danger of frost had passed he always propped the lid open to keep the heat from building up on the inside and killing the plants.

* * *

While Dad didn't love cucumbers, he did love cabbage. He loved coleslaw and homemade sauerkraut. He loved cooked cabbage and ham. He loved sauerkraut with pork chops or sausages, so he grew a lot of cabbage. After the young cabbage plants were two or three inches high in the cold frame, he would set them into the garden. He set each plant into the ground and then forced a rusty old coffee can with both ends cut out over the transplant to a depth of an inch or two. This was to keep cutworms from cutting the roots. It's pretty devastating to set out cabbage plants and come back in a day or two to find many of them wilted and lying on the ground. If that happened, he'd take his finger and trench the soil around the plant, looking for the culprit. There it would be—a fat worm curled into a tight C–a miserable, disgusting pest. The cans seemed to stop the cabbage slaughter.

The next pests Dad had to fight were cabbage moths. He tried a lot of different applications to keep the moths from laying eggs and producing larvae that chewed away at the leaves of the forming cabbage heads. One of those applications was dish soap and honey. The dish soap was distasteful to the bugs, and the honey made it stick to the plant. It was moderately successful. The real success came from the length of the growing days. Summer days were fourteen to sixteen hours long, and the cabbage simply grew faster than the bugs could eat it. At any rate, by harvest time the cabbage plants would be four feet across with the cabbage heads weighing up to fifteen pounds. He'd watch those swelling heads like a hawk and, just when they began to split, he'd harvest them.

* * *

For a long time Dad didn't grow asparagus, but then he took a notion that he'd like to do so. Did he go to the store and buy roots? Oh, no. He watched along the road where asparagus had gone wild, dug it up, and transplanted it to his garden. He put it out beside the greenhouse in an area where he'd throw garden refuse—a kind of informal compost pit. The asparagus loved it, and we had all the asparagus we could eat. He'd chop it up raw and add it to salads. He'd freeze some, but mostly it was eaten as quickly as it came up. Later in the season he'd stop cutting it and let it go to seed. It would produce huge fernlike plants that eventually produced a few red berries. Pretty, but useless.

Dad was never very successful at growing strawberries, though he tried several times. Probably the soil was too alkaline to produce good berries. It was also somewhat discouraging that the minute the berries would ripen, the robins would swoop down and eat them all. While he never did well with strawberries, he did great with raspberries. He harvested so many raspberries from a couple of rows of vines that we had to pick them every other day. They were small and tasty and wonderful either in a bowl with cream and sugar on top or made into jam.

* * *

Most people were horrified when they saw how Dad thinned his garden. He thinned carrots to an inch to two inches apart. He set cabbage out a couple of feet apart. He planted radishes, beans, corn, and squash seeds with plenty of space between them. Beets, kohlrabi, and rutabagas met the same fate as the carrots—Dad thinned them severely when the plants put out their second set of leaves. He knew what he was doing, and soon the long sunny days, great soil, and adequate water had those plants pushing each other for space. Then, he'd thin again. This time he'd start taking out every other plant for the dinner table or to give away. He had a philosophy that if you pulled one out and gave it away, the two remaining plants would grow together.

Dad was generous to a fault and would give to anyone who asked with pleasure. He was not so excited about garden raiders—usually kids—who just wanted to see if they could get by with stealing a few carrots. However, there were a few occasions when reports were that there were adults in the garden with big long knives harvesting full heads of cabbage. He never could understand why people would steal cabbage when it is one of the least expensive vegetables to buy.

* * *

Weather in Montana can be exceedingly brutal, and only the tough can survive there—tough plants and tough people. There is not much more discouraging than to have a garden up, thinned, and growing like crazy, and then have thick black clouds roll in and know that within minutes it could be hailing. Dad knew when it was going to hail. He understood the weather conditions so well that he knew. Sometimes, before it began to hail, we could hear the hail rolling in the clouds above—a grinding sound that's not quite like thunder. Then it was time to watch out and take cover. Usually, there wasn't time for much of anything except to pray the garden would be spared.

Hail, when it came, could be anywhere from pea-sized pellets to baseball-sized stones. There were times when the hail lay two to three inches deep after a storm—cold, icy, destructive piles of it. As soon as it stopped, Dad would be out in the garden to survey the damage. There were times when the hail had driven most of the young plants right into the ground. There were other times when the plants still stood, though their leaves were tattered and torn. If the hail came early in the season, and if it was severe enough to destroy the seedlings, he had time to replant. But usually those storms came in mid-July when it was too late. Sometimes those battered relics of what had been thriving vegetables would struggle up out of the damage and begin to grow again. They'd do fairly well, though it was never the bumper crops he'd hoped for.

Dad would leave the parsnips in the ground all winter. Then he would dig them from the frozen soil and bring them to the house. Mom would fry them in butter. One time when he was out digging parsnips, a young boy came along and watched. Soon he asked, "Mister, do you have vegetables growing in your garden?" Dad laughed and tried to explain, but one can only imagine what that child told his parents when he got home.

* * *

Dad had begun his gardening days by helping his physically disabled mother in her garden when he was only a young boy. Gardening was in his blood. In fact, sometimes it seemed as though it *was* his lifeblood. A few days before he died, he was in his last garden, giving his grandsons-in-law pointers on how to grow vegetables. There he was with a weeder in his hand, and there stood the young men with notepads, taking down every word of wisdom. His garden was one of his great joys in life, and when our family sat down to eat, more often than not he'd say, "God is good. Just look at this table. Everything on it except for the salt and butter came from our own hands." His satisfaction was in knowing he had provided at a most basic level for those entrusted to his care with his own hands and by his own efforts.

20

Skippy

I suppose in every lifetime there is one special animal that makes a lasting impression. In my life, that animal was Skippy. We didn't adopt him. He adopted us.

My mom was working as an accountant at the Ford Motor Company in Deer Lodge, Montana. One day, one of the company's salesmen came in from the car lot complaining about a dog that kept getting into the cars and sleeping on the seats. Mom went to see what they were talking about. She found a black-and-white fox terrier mix right where the salesman said it would be—asleep in a car. He appeared to be healthy, friendly, and intelligent. She went back inside and called my dad to see if she could bring him home. I think Daddy was reluctant, but he finally said yes.

When she arrived home that evening, the dog was with her. We named him "Skippy." He settled right in, just as if he'd always been with us. Daddy's reluctance about having a pet melted away immediately. Within a few days, the two became fast friends, and they stayed friends for many, many years until Skippy's death.

Skippy was probably the most intelligent animal I have ever known. And he had soul too. If you praised him, he got it right away. If you shamed him, he got that right away as well. He knew lots of tricks and learned them after being shown how to do them only a few times. When he arrived at our house, he was skinny, smelled bad, and was extremely tired. He was assigned a place under the kitchen counter where he could sleep. It was right in the middle of the family's activities, yet he was out of the way. He liked his place immediately and went willingly to his rug at the end of each day.

After we'd had Skippy for a time, my brother acquired some rabbits. One day, one of the expectant mother rabbits got out of the hutch and delivered her babies in some soft grass near the garage. We didn't know she had gotten out of the hutch, but Skippy did. Fox terriers didn't get their names by lying on silken pillows in a king's palace somewhere. They are hunting dogs and will go into a barking frenzy when chasing prey.

Skippy came to the house to get Daddy. He fussed and whined and stewed. He followed at Daddy's heels until Daddy finally turned to him and said, "What is it? Do you want me to follow you?" Skippy jumped around, ran a few feet in the direction of the garage, and came back. "All right, I'm coming," Daddy told the worried dog who was already running toward the garage. *What in the world does he want?* Daddy thought.

Skippy ran straight to a pile of tiny naked baby rabbits with their eyes sealed tight and bulging in their tiny skulls. He could have killed all of them at the same time with one bite. Instead, he stood whining and looking at Dad. "Well, I'll be . . ." Daddy said. He took off his cap and carefully lifted the babies into it. He carried them back to the hutch. It didn't take long to locate the mother rabbit, catch her, and return her to the safety of her cage. Skippy had denied his natural hunting instincts to rescue the baby rabbits.

That experience taught us a lot about our little dog. Later on, we understood how truly amazing it was that he had sought help for the baby bunnies. We were coming home from an outing in our pickup truck when a huge jackrabbit dashed in front of us. Jackrabbits are big rabbits about a foot tall, and they have ears that are about another foot long. They look gigantic. Daddy stopped the car as the rabbit ran to the side of the road. Skippy saw the rabbit too. He leapt out the window and chased after that jackrabbit. We got out of the truck and called and called. He either didn't hear us or didn't want to hear us. The last thing we saw was a jackrabbit disappearing over the hill followed closely by a frantic black-and-white fox terrier.

We kids were very upset. We figured we had seen the last of our dog. We called and called, but there was no answer. We had just about given up when a head poked up over the horizon. It was Skippy. He had come back to see if we were still there. This time when we called him, he took one last look in the direction the rabbit had disappeared and then came trotting back down the hill to us. He was hot and panting. He crawled into the car, laid down on the floor by an air vent, and was very still the rest of the way home. We knew then that his natural instinct was to give chase, which made the miracle of his protecting the baby rabbits even more amazing.

Neighbors who lived two doors down the street got a collie pup. The collie's name was . . . you guessed it . . . Lassie. We watched her grow from a roly-poly puppy to a golden, longhaired adult collie. She was beautiful. She and Skippy became fast friends. Every day she would come to the window of our dining room, stick her nose against the glass, and grin. We would let Skippy out, and they would roughhouse and tumble all over the yard with the glee of a couple of young kids let out of school.

That went on for a couple of years. Then one day, once again, Skippy started bugging Daddy to get his attention. He whined and ran a few feet and came back. By this time, Daddy was well trained. He turned to Skippy and said, "What's wrong? Do you want me to follow you?" Skippy let him know that he did. Daddy followed Skippy to the neighbor's yard. There lay Lassie. She had been hit by a car and was dying. Skippy had done the only thing he knew how to do to help a friend. He had run home to get someone he could trust and had brought him to her. Skippy grieved Lassie's death. He never did have another friend like her.

Skippy liked to help. When Daddy planted potatoes in the early spring, he dug holes in the ground and dropped in the pieces of potatoes that would grow into plants. One day, when Daddy was halfway down a row of potatoes, he looked behind him. There was Skippy, covering up every piece of potato and filling every hole. Another time he and Daddy had gone to the neighbors' house. The neighbors had given Daddy a package of frozen meat. On the way home, Skippy wanted to help and was pestering Dad to let him carry the package. So Daddy gave it to him. The dog got quite a shock when the frozen package was thrust into his mouth. He dropped it. Daddy said, "No, you wanted to carry it, now you take it!" Skippy grabbed the frozen package and ran as hard as he could for the house, where he deposited it at the back door. He never asked again.

One time, Daddy was repairing the roof of our house. He was way out on the front eave and twenty-five feet from the ground. He was concentrating on his work when something warm and wet touched his neck. It's a wonder he didn't fall off the roof. Slowly, he turned his head to see what had touched him. There stood Skippy, wagging his tail. He had climbed the ladder, crawled over the ridge of the house, and now stood next to Daddy. He'd come to help, but he couldn't climb down the ladder. Daddy had to get up carefully, pick up the dog, climb back down the slope of the roof, and then down the ladder. In the future, he pulled the ladder up on the roof to keep Skippy from climbing it.

* * *

At a nearby lake, there was a ramshackle Boy Scout camp. A church group once held a youth retreat there. Daddy was the chief cook and bottle washer. There were some very interesting innovations in that place. One of them was a system for heating water. Outside the kitchen, there was a fifty-gallon barrel set up on bricks to act as a boiler. Above the camp was a spring. The Boy Scouts had piped water down the hill and into the barrel. To heat the water, one had to build a fire under the boiler, and from there it ran into the main building where most of the activities took place. One time we got the fire too hot. When we turned on the sink tap, steam came out. That was not a good plan. Fortunately, no one was hurt.

Daddy and the young men slept in that big old building, and Skippy stayed with them. Some of the floorboards were getting old and had holes and gaps between them. Skippy found a hole with a rat's nest under it. Although no one ever saw a rat or even a mouse, Skippy decided to stand guard at that hole in the floor. He stood there for three days and two nights. Perhaps he's the reason no one ever saw a rat. Finally, it was time to go home. You can believe we had one exhausted dog in our truck. He slept most of the short way home.

When we got home, he went straight to his bed under the kitchen counter and immediately fell asleep. He didn't want to get up for anything—not to eat, not to drink, and not even to go outside to do his business. Mom would rouse him a couple of times a day. She almost had to carry him outside. As soon as he was finished with his business, he'd come back inside and crawl into his bed. He slept for three days and nights before he was his old self again.

One day when we were in the garage—the one with the charred interior—we discovered a mouse behind the cardboard. We sicced Skippy on it, but he couldn't get it. He began grabbing the cardboard in his teeth and tearing it off the walls. He worked and worked. Of course, the mouse was long gone before he got anywhere near it. We were continually amazed by his ability to solve problems.

But perhaps one of the most poignant moments of this little dog's amazing activities came when we were on a vacation. Skippy never stayed in a kennel. He went everywhere with us. We were in Minnesota when my brother Glen became ill. He was so sick that we feared for his life. No one knew what was wrong with him. The doctors in town suggested Mom and Dad take him to the Mayo Clinic in Rochester—which was nearby. They took him there, and he was hospitalized. Ray and

I stayed with my aunt. We silently prowled around her house, too afraid to talk about what was happening to our brother.

When Mom and Dad came home from the hospital that first night, they needed to pray about this desperate situation. They looked for a place to pray and for others who would pray with them. They found a small congregation that gladly joined them in prayer for my brother. There was no fanfare or calls from the hospital with good news that his condition was improved, but when my parents came back from prayer, Mom said, "I know he will be all right." And he was.

The next morning when they returned to the hospital, miraculously, Glen was sitting up and working jigsaw puzzles. After a few more days in the hospital for recovery and observation, he was released. His diagnosis was mumps meningitis/encephalitis. The doctors thought Mom and Daddy would have to get an ambulance to take Glen home to Montana—a distance of 1,000 miles. It just so happened that we had that homemade camper on the back of the pickup truck we were traveling in. The doctors thought that as long as Glen could lie down, it would be all right for him to go home that way.

We loaded up the truck and headed for the hospital. Mom and Dad went in and signed the papers so that Glen could be released. Then they brought him out in a wheelchair. When Daddy opened the door to the back of the camper, Skippy saw Glen. Ray and I held onto his collar with all our might as Skippy strained to reach Glen. Skippy had known all along that something was wrong. He knew someone was missing. He knew that being together with his family—his whole family—was just about the best thing that could happen to a small black-and-white fox terrier.

Skippy died long after all of us kids had grown up and left home. Now, when we return to Montana, we can almost see him out chasing rabbits, helping Daddy plant potatoes, or wagging his tail furiously in absolute delight that we have come home. He will always be alive in our hearts.

21

Watermelons in the Snow

High in the mountains above the little farming village of Gold Creek, Montana, are some small lakes simply called "Gold Creek Lakes." We didn't go to the Gold Creek Lakes very often when I was a child for several reasons. One was that getting there was difficult. Another was that the fishing wasn't very good. The third was that there were other places that were friendlier to family camping. Because of all of this, a trip to Gold Creek Lakes became very special.

Shortly after leaving the little town of Gold Creek (hardly more than a post office and a small cluster of buildings), our vehicle—either the four-wheeled Jeep station wagon we had for a while or a pickup with a mysterious gear called "compound"—climbed almost straight up over rocks and washed-out roads. There were places where the brush had grown so close to the "road" that there was an almost continuous swishing sound on the side of the vehicle as the leafy branches scraped it. The way up was beautiful. It was green, verdant, cool, and wonderful. Sometimes the road looked more like creek bed with water running freely down the middle of it. About halfway up there was an old placer operation. Miners, searching for the ever-elusive gold, had stripped the landscape, washing away the soil and leaving behind piles of rocks.

In placer mining, workers use high-pressure water hoses to wash down the side of a hill and expose the gold. Then they run the soil and rocks through a series of sluice boxes to separate the gold from the soil. The operation always leaves behind acres and acres of rocks piled up in giant mountains. Most of the soil washes away, and it will be thousands of years before the land recovers, if ever. This desolate area was the exact opposite of the lush area we had just traversed. It was ugly, and I always felt a sense of despair at what had been done to the landscape.

At last we arrived at a kind of campsite. It was little more than a turnaround on this steep dead-end road, and it was hard to find a level place to set up a table. Most times Dad figured out a way to park the pickup with the camper fairly level. And if it wasn't exactly level, he would encourage us to sleep with our heads uphill so the blood wouldn't flow to our heads and make us dizzy when we got up. We didn't need anything else to make us dizzy, as the altitude of the place (at 7,260 feet) could do that all on its own. It was high up, and it could be very cool—all right, cold—right in the middle of summer.

I remember taking one trip to Gold Creek Lakes around the Fourth of July. Even though the air was warm, there were snow banks all around. We had brought along a huge watermelon to eat. While we were unpacking, Mom said, "Where are we going to put this watermelon?" Dad picked it up, walked away, and with a great heave threw it right into the middle of the snow bank. Then he shoveled snow over the top. We would be eating icy-cold watermelon. Yum! The next day after one of our exploring excursions, we returned to find tire tracks within inches of our watermelon. Someone had come up the road and used the space where the watermelon was buried as a turnaround. We nearly had squished watermelon.

* * *

I am sure Daddy knew every spring in Powell County and probably beyond that as well. We'd be with him somewhere out in the woods and start to complain about being thirsty. He'd get this far-away thinking kind of look in his eyes. If the water source he had remembered was a long way off, he'd encourage us to get in the car, and we'd drive to the spring. But often when he'd get that look we'd start off hiking. When we arrived at our destination, he'd sweep away the brush with his big hand and long arm, and there would be crystal-clear water bubbling right up from the ground.

At Gold Creek Lakes, the spring was just down a short trail. We'd get our buckets and a cup and go there for water. Dad was forever trying to keep us kids from stirring up the silt in the bottom of the pool and muddying the water. The spring was shallow, and the pool it formed was about three feet across. Talk about good water! The only problem was that it was *so* cold it would make your teeth ache and your esophagus feel like a frozen Popsicle.

There were two lakes. One was just called Gold Creek Lake, and the other was Rainbow Lake. Rainbow Lake was my favorite, but to get there we had to walk about a quarter of a mile over a little hill. From where the truck was parked, we walked up a rocky footpath, crawled over a few downed logs, and crossed the crest of the hill to descend into a lot of brush. Scrubby willow trees all but obscured the path, and we had to be very careful not to miss the trail. The only time as a child I ever felt panic running loose in the woods was in those willows when I lost the trail for a couple of minutes.

Both lakes are cirque lakes, which means the walls surrounding them were carved out of solid rock in a circular fashion by glacial action. On the side where we approached Rainbow Lake were boulders pushed out into the water. We'd put down towels and jackets on the rocks for padding so we could lie on them and soak up a little warmth from the sun. But try as I might, I could never get things arranged in a way that made lying there comfortable. On the other side of the lake was a sheer wall of rock, and below it was a huge landslide of scree (loose rock broken in small pieces and spilled down the mountainside). One could go around the lake on a very primitive path and even cross the rockslide, but only the most determined fishermen did so.

One time when we walked over to Rainbow Lake, my brothers and I found that receding snow had left a pool of water in a depression in the ground. It was a fairly large body of water. The bottom of the pond was lined with long grass that had grown there the summer before, dried, and then been covered with snow. The snow had melted, and the depression had filled with water. The water, standing in the intense Montana sun, was warm. We decided it would be a great place to wade—much better than the frigid water of the lake. Off came our shoes, and then we discovered that the bog was full of baby frogs. It looked to us as if there were about a million of them.

We got the red plastic bucket that seemed to accompany us on every camping trip, started catching frogs, and then put them in the bucket. We probably had a hundred or so in there. We were having a ball splashing about in bathtub-warm water, catching slippery frogs an inch or so long. When we tired of the game, it seemed defeating to simply dump the frogs back where we found them. So we poured the pail of frogs and the water into that bitterly cold lake. Frogs are cold-blooded aren't they? I hope so, because if they weren't they probably died of heart failure.

When we told Dad, who had been fishing, about our escapades, he was reminded of his own frog adventures. Daddy had spent the last part of his childhood in Washington State, where his dad had bought a stump farm. A "stump farm" was an area that had been logged off and the huge cedar and Douglas fir stumps left in the ground. The only way the land could be farmed was to clear the stumps. You did this by blasting them loose and then dragging them out with a team of horses or a tractor. It was miserable backbreaking work, and my grandfather expected his two strapping pre-teen sons to help.

They did, but they were still kids and did kid things. One time they found a bunch of slippery, slimy frog eggs. They got a bucket, scooped them up, and took them to a hole that had been left when a stump had been pulled from the ground. The hole had filled with water from the constant rain for which western Washington is famous. The boys poured the slimy mass in the hole and promptly forgot about it. Later, when Grandpa and his sons went out to start pulling stumps again, they happened by that hole in the ground. It was teeming with about ten thousand tadpoles. Of course, none of them survived, because that many tadpoles used up all the oxygen in the water. It became a stinking mess and a good learning experience to let Mother Nature do things her own way.

Glen and Ray did their own frog egg experiment many years later. The rest of the family knew nothing about the jars of frog eggs they had stored in the shed. But one day Dad was looking for something on his workbench and saw these containers of something indescribable. He picked one up and held it to the light. He vaguely remembered the gelatinous mass he and his brother had poured in the stump hole, and after a short kindly lecture about what happens to frog eggs that are trapped without air in an artificial environment, he dumped the whole stinking mess in the garbage can.

* * *

Sometimes when you're a kid, you grouse and complain about the discomforts of things like camping. Sometimes you think childhood will never end, and then suddenly it's all over. There are wonderful places you don't go to anymore, and there are people you loved who are gone, and you know that an era has passed. In that moment you are grateful for the experiences and the loving people who made them possible—and you begin to think how you could pass those experiences on to your own children and their kids.

2 2

Fish Stories

"You can't catch fish if you don't put your hook in the water," Dad used to tell my brothers. It is as true of life as it was of fishing. Going fishing in the crystal-clear waters of Montana's rivers was as much a part of our life there as was going to school. I'm sure for Dad it was one more way he could provide for his family, but no one was fooled. For him it wasn't just about providing food for our table. He loved wading in hip-high rubber boots in those icy, glacial-fed streams. He loved snaking the tip of a long fly cast into the stream and under a bank of willows where he knew "Old Wiley" was hiding.

He used to say, "God doesn't count the days you spend fishing when he's figuring up how long you should live." There's truth in that saying. When the pressures became too great, Dad would get out the fly rod and boots. He'd soon back the pickup out of the driveway, calling, "I'm just going down to the Little Blackfoot for a while before dark," and off he'd go. Sometimes he'd come back with a creel loaded with fish. Other times there might be one or two fish or even nothing, but always he was relaxed.

Another favorite fishing spot of the town folks was Rock Creek. I don't know why *this* little stream had the privilege of being named "Rock Creek," as every creek in our valley was lined with round, smooth glacial rocks. But that was its name, and it was a favorite place for our family. It, too, was very close to the house. We'd go west and then north on an old gravel road that began right where Kentucky Street bent to become Milwaukee Avenue. That was the Old Stage Coach Road between Deer Lodge and the town of Gold Creek. We'd go west for three or four miles, past Smiling Pool, past the Hillcrest Cemetery, past an old homestead, past some sheep sheds, and then turn north still following the same road.

First we'd climb a not-very-high but rather steep hill. On the other side of that hill was a gully that was truly impressive. We called it Mullen's Gulch. We wound down the hill to the bottom, crossed a little murky stream, and then Dad would shift down the truck gears to climb up the other side. Soon after climbing out of that gully, we'd turn west again. We'd soon arrive at Rock Creek, where we would fish until dark.

We ate so many rainbow trout when I was growing up that there were times in the summer when I thought I couldn't swallow one more bite. When we'd complain, we'd get a pep talk about fish being brain food and how lucky we were to have them. I didn't believe it until I was grown and saw what restaurants charged for trout. I've eaten very few trout since then.

I don't suppose anything tastes much better than fresh fish fried in a cast-iron skillet over a campfire. Mom had a way of rolling the fish in flour and cornmeal and then frying them real crispy on one side before turning them over to fry crispy on the other side. Then she'd dish the golden brown fish onto our plates, add some pan-fried potatoes and sliced tomatoes, and we had a meal fit for a king.

While Mom took the heads off for frying, she always left the tail on the fish. That gave you something to hang onto when separating the meat from bones. We quickly learned how to do that by holding the fish up by the tail and inserting a tine of the fork through the skin and meat. Then we could carefully tease the meat away from the skeleton. When done this way, there were few bones left in the fish except near the dorsal fin on the back and a few others near the little fins on the underside.

Dad carried an old wicker creel with grass tucked into it. When he was fishing, he'd periodically wet the creel and grass in the stream to keep the fish as fresh as possible. When he came into the kitchen after a fishing trip, he'd head straight for the sink and fill it with water. Then he'd reach into the creel and take the fish out one by one as we gathered around to see what he'd caught. Although I got tired of eating fish, I never got tired of seeing what he brought home. And usually there was a story to go with each fish.

We kids would push the fish under the water and feel the slimy slickness of their skin. In just a few minutes we'd have to step out of the way, because Dad had finished sharpening a knife on his whetstone and was ready to clean them. I can't say that the smell of fish guts is my favorite in the world, but I can say it is distinctive. It's not a foul smell, just distinctive. I can still see Dad's great big hand holding up a fish belly. He'd insert a knife near the tail and cut all the way to the gills. Than he'd stick his big finger into the fish's mouth and open it wide to expose the thin flesh beneath the gills. By inserting his knife all the way through this paper-thin flesh, he could strip away the intestines in one pull from jaw to tail.

We always wanted to see what was inside the fish. I was fascinated when a fish was full of orange-yellow rubbery eggs. Dad would show us the liver, and sometimes in a big fish we'd find a little fish that had been its dinner. Dad would then scrape the skin with the flat of the knife to remove the slime and some of the scales. Finally, he'd slit the membrane that held the spinal fluid and clean all that out. After thoroughly rinsing the fish, they were ready either for supper the next day or to be put in the freezer to be eaten during winter. One trick Mom and Dad had was to freeze fish completely submerged in water to prevent freezer burn and shriveling of the flesh.

Sometimes when I'm hungry for something I can't identify, I think back to those pan-fried fish and long to sink my teeth into that pale pink flesh. And it doesn't matter to me at all whether it is brain food or not.

23

A Skinny Black Cat

I came home from school one day to find Daddy sitting in the grass in the backyard holding the skinniest coal black cat I had ever seen. Its tail was longer than the cat. "Look what came to see us," he said, looking up. He knew I would be delighted, because I loved animals. "It's a little female cat, and she's really hungry."

We started feeding her, and she could really pack it away. It seemed she just couldn't get enough. We kids were delighted. We had a new pet.

Sunday night came, and we went to church as we always did. After church we usually went straight home unless there was a party at the church. Once in a while someone would invite us over for dessert, but usually we went straight home and ate ice cream or cereal.

Well, on this particular Sunday night when we came home, something attracted Dad's attention to the woodshed. The shed was only a few feet from the house. Just inside the door that stood perpetually ajar, Daddy had built a box along one wall where he raised baby chicks. In that box, when it was not in use as a chicken starting box, we stored various and sundry things. There were some old rags in there. Well, this night, Dad went in and pulled the string in the middle of the room to turn on the light. The light flared in the darkness, almost blinding us.

"Well, would you look here," he said, surprised at something. There in the chicken box were six baby kittens and that long, skinny coal-black mother. The kittens were not newborns, either—they had their eyes open and were quite mobile. That cat had carried those six babies in her mouth one at a time from wherever they had been born to a safe place where she had found food and love. There she was, with trust in her actions and in her eyes.

We kids had more fun with those kittens than you can imagine. We teased them for one thing, not realizing they might become uncontrollable. And they did—become uncontrollable. You could not walk across the lawn without one of them charging across the yard and attaching itself to your leg. I guess I would have to call that season "the summer of the scratches." Our legs and arms wore the continual scars of mortal battle with felines.

In the fall when the weather began to grow cold, Momma Kitty and most of her babies mysteriously disappeared. I imagine my father, fearing a proliferation of cats, had taken most of them and disposed of them. (I didn't ask questions then, and I don't want to know now. Daddy was strong, and even though he was tenderhearted, he did what had to be done—always.)

There were two little black-and-white boy cats left, and we took them inside and to our hearts. They were more than playful; they were a nuisance with their play. They would get so wild and unapproachable that we would have to take a blanket, throw it over them, roll up the blanket with them in it, and take them to the door where we dumped them outside in the snow to cool off. When they came back in, they were much mellower.

One day, one of them decided to play with a ball of red yarn. He rolled and chased and rolled some more and thoroughly wound himself up in it until he could not move. I don't know how, but Mom managed to cut him out of his dilemma. There was no way he could be unwound, so she just had to take the scissors to the yarn. I imagine she came away with some pretty serious scratches from trying to free him.

These were just a few animals in a long line of pets. Somewhere deep inside me, I must have carried a memory of them, for I love black-and-white cats. I have had three of my own: Charles Dickens, Tiny Tim, and Whiskers.

24

The Big Blackfoot River

We all loved the Big Blackfoot River. Daddy especially loved its broad, crystal-clear waters that ran first through the Scapegoat Wilderness and then through the valleys and farmlands of northern Powell County past Lincoln and Helmville. The rainbow and cutthroat trout in that river could reach three to four pounds, and the meat was both firm and tender. The water in the Big Blackfoot ran right out of a glacier somewhere above, and it stayed cold all summer long. The bed of the Blackfoot River up in the Scapegoat Wilderness was paved with dark pink- and bluish-colored stones. It looked as if the water was flowing over some kind of elaborate mosaic.

There was a seven-mile trek along the North Fork of the Big Blackfoot River into the Scapegoat Wilderness. At the trailhead was an encampment for horses and pack mules for those who chose to ride into the backcountry. But it was possible to hike back to the North Fork as well. Several times Daddy and various people hiked in to fish, and, oh, the stories they would tell when they came back in two or three days! But the one I remember most was the story of Glen's miraculous escape from death.

Glen was finally old enough and strong enough to make the five-day trip. He and Dad fished up and down the river as they went into the wilderness. That area had lots of scree, and the loose rocks were slippery and tricky to walk on. Well, Glen was walking along on the scree when he evidently stepped on a key rock holding a whole lot of rocks in place. When he stepped on it, the whole mountainside above him came to life and started to slide. He tripped and fell into a hollow space beside a large rock.

There Glen stayed while the rocks bounced all around him. Daddy had seen what was happening and ran down the river to be there if Glen was knocked into the river. When the slide stopped, there was Glen, terrified, but unharmed. God had hidden him in a safe place while the devastation rained down all around him. Daddy didn't even get his feet wet.

I didn't go to the Scapegoat Wilderness until I was grown and my children were old enough to carry their own packs. Then I went twice. We took our time hiking to the wilderness camp—seven miles in. Our family had been doing a lot of hiking, so we were up for the trip. We pretty much followed the Big Blackfoot River all the way to the camp. It was a beautiful walk with lush greenery along the trail, and there was always the possibility we would meet wildlife.

On this trip, I remember that Mom, the kids, and I were cleaning fish on a rocky beach along the river when we looked up to discover we had a visitor—a black, furry, snuffling visitor who had smelled our fish and come to investigate. The black bear was on a bank across the river. It's one thing to be in a place where you can retreat from a bear to a vehicle and watch from inside, but it's quite another thing to be seven miles from your car with no place to hide. We just hoped the racket we were making was enough to keep the predator at bay. (Actually, most American black bears are afraid of humans and will do anything they can to avoid them. It is only in parks where they have been taught to beg that they become a fearless nuisance.) After a few minutes, the bear ambled off, and we quietly made our retreat.

It was on this trip, too, that my son, Mark, caught his first fish. He and Grandpa went up the river a bit while the rest of us ate our lunch and relaxed. Pretty soon the two returned, and Mark had a fairly nice-sized trout.

When we got to camp that first evening, Mark and my daughter, Wendy, were playing and trying to find something to do. Ever resourceful, they went off into the woods—close enough so we could hear their voices and know they were all right. They came back once to ask if they could borrow a tarp that Dad had brought along. Then there was more whispering and fussing around in the woods. Pretty soon we heard someone coming, and we looked up to see a seven-foot-tall creature with a black beard, wearing a cape and a fez of some sort. Our first thought was, *What in the world?* Then we recognized the tarp.

There was Mark, up on Wendy's shoulders with a stocking cap on his head, the tarp wrapped around his shoulders. He had a beard of black lichen that they had pulled off a tree and attached to his face with pitch. We laughed ourselves silly. The only problem was that we didn't have anything to remove that pitch at the end of the show. It just had to wear off Mark's face and Wendy's fingers.

* * *

It was on that trip that Mark almost scared me to death. The river was broad at that point—probably sixty to 100 feet wide—and moved very quickly. I was standing on a horse bridge and wearing a visor hat. The wind caught it and it was gone in seconds, riding the current of the river around a bend and out of sight. Well, we were standing on the horse bridge when Mark climbed over the railing. What I saw was his head disappearing over the edge. I screamed and ran to the railing. I thought he was gone forever. What I didn't know was that there was a broad piling that formed a substantial platform. He was quite safe and had a good laugh at my consternation. But he decided that he'd better not scare me like that again.

I had another scare on that trip, but it wasn't the terrified kind Mark had given me. It was a dread that my mother was going to push her luck too far once too often. She was the kind of woman who liked to go to the top of every mountain — as high as possible. She liked to go off hunting by herself. She often had what to me would have been scary adventures. This time it was all about taking pictures.

We hiked up a trail to see a waterfall. The view from the trail did not give us a good view of the falls, so Mom leaned out over the edge of a crumbly cliff to take a picture. I was sure she was either going to fall off the cliff or the cliff was going to crumble and send her plunging about fifty feet to the bottom of the falls. Neither happened, but I still cringe when I think of her hanging out into open space taking pictures.

* * *

The trip up the Blackfoot that I remember most was the one we took a couple of years later. My brother, Ray, and his family were in Montana at the same time as our family. We decided we would all hike to the Forest Service campground and spend a couple of nights. There were five in Ray's family, four in ours, and Mom and Dad. The oldest kids were in junior high, and the youngest was about seven years old. So they were old enough to walk and carry a small daypack.

Dad was very concerned about taking all of us into the backcountry where grizzly bears and black bears were a concern. He decided he better take a rifle. So, in addition to his well-laden pack, he carried a gun for protection. It was a heavy load. Mom carried about a thirty-five pound pack. She was a tough Montana woman.

We tried to stay together as we walked up the trail. It took all day long, but when we arrived in the evening, we got a fire going. All cooking had to be done over an open fire — we couldn't really carry a camp stove to a place like that. Our family had a four-man, ten-pound backpack tent we had purchased for a trip to Europe. Mom and Dad had a tiny two-man tent. We set them up. Ray and his family decided they wanted to sleep outdoors under the stars.

In the evening, Ray's family walked over to the ranger station. There was no one there, as the station was more of a way station to feed and water horses on treks into the backcountry than it was an actual destination. There was a lot of dry hay lying around on the ground, so Ray and his family gathered arms full of it to cushion their hips and shoulders against the hard, cold ground. They spread the hay beside a fallen log so that when they lay down in their sleeping bags, their heads were toward the log—a kind of primitive headboard.

We ate and sat around telling stories until we were sleepy. I don't think I ever saw Mom any happier than she was on that trip. Two of her children and five of her grandchildren were with her in a place she loved almost more than any other location on earth. She chattered away happily. Then it was time for bed.

Mom and Dad crawled into their little blue-and-white tent. Our family went to the four-man tent. Ray's family bedded down outside. It was a great idea until the middle of the night, when I awoke to thunder and the gentle pitter-patter of rain. I crawled out of my sleeping bag and unzipped the tent. There were people scurrying all over the place in the pitch dark.

"In here, get in here!" I yelled. In seconds, sleeping bags, bits of hay, clothing, and who-knows-what were being thrown into the tent. Then the bodies started piling in—one, two, three—which meant there were seven of us in a four-man tent (and I often questioned if that meant four full-sized men or four little people). Ray's son, Rolf, fell into the tent with Mom and Dad. Ray decided to ride out the storm under a tree. (Looking back and knowing what I now know about lightning, that wasn't a particularly wise choice, but he survived.)

We had no idea what time it was, but it was on the morning side of the night. Since the sun comes up at about 4:30 AM in the summer in Montana, it wasn't too long till dawn. But believe me, it was long enough.

For many years as children, we had joked about so many people sleeping in a bed that they fit together like a stack of spoons. When one wanted to turn over, he or she had to say, "spoon!" Then the whole group would turn at once. Well, believe it or not, there were so many of us in that tent that someone actually called out "spoon," and we all rolled over. If I hadn't been so exhausted from walking seven miles carrying a pack and then being rudely interrupted in my sleep, I would have split my sides laughing. But a simple chuckle had to suffice.

Finally it was morning, and I crawled out. After a while, I watched the tent disgorge body after body. Dad was out and had a fire going. Everything was soggy, but the sun came up bright and warm. We started spreading wet sleeping bags and clothing over trees, rocks, and any place we thought they might dry. We had stuff spread out over about a fifty square-foot area. As the sun warmed the items, they started to steam. What a mess!

Then the stories started. Daddy said they had unzipped their tent and Rolf plus a lot of clothing had come flying in. In the morning when he woke up, he wondered what he had tangled around his head and discovered it was his daughter-in-law's bra.

Along about noon, a ranger wandered up. Our clothing and sleeping bags were starting to dry, and Ray had turned the hay once or twice to dry it. We were loafing around, drinking coffee and talking when the ranger came. He sat down and chatted with us for a while, and then looked around surveying the devastation we had caused in his forest. "You will clean this up when you leave, won't you?" he asked. We assured him we would. After he left, we roared with laughter as we looked around and saw the site as he must have seen it.

The second night went better, and after a good night's sleep we cleaned up the camp and even carried the hay back to the ranger's station. We started back down the trail. There were groups in front eager to get back down the trail and groups in the back dawdling along. Somehow, I got separated from everyone and found myself walking along totally alone for about twenty minutes. It was a wonderful and slightly scary experience to be all alone in the woods. There was only the sound of a gentle breeze sighing in the trees and the babble of the river. The only fear I had was that around the next corner I might meet a bear or a moose. Nothing else really scared me, and, of course, I didn't meet anything. I soon met the others resting by the bridge. We kept together the rest of the way.

When we at last got back to the cars, we had this great sense of an adventure that had come off very well. And when I took off my heavy backpack, I thought I was going to fall on my face. The release from the load unbalanced me. After a few minutes we all adjusted and then went home to the house in Deer Lodge, happy and thankful that we had tucked a lot more memories into our memory bank.

25

Riot!

Visitors were always amazed when they entered Deer Lodge from the south end of town and saw a huge castle-like fortress sitting on the main street of town. Its twenty-five foot high walls abutted the sidewalk. Its towers were spaced along the walls. A huge front gate and entry door were made of solid steel. The Montana State Penitentiary was too close, too real, and too much a part of our lives to be ignored. It was referred to locally as "The Big House."

The penitentiary had been built in the 1800s by convict labor to house all of Montana's criminals. Its walls of massive blocks of gray stone encompassed acres of land. Inside the stone walls were two huge, red brick buildings—cell blocks. Invisible from the outside were other buildings of industry and supply for the prison. There was a laundry, a license plate factory, an infirmary, a theater, and a large exercise yard. There was a ball diamond just outside the walls where "trustees" could play softball behind a twelve-foot high fence topped with barbed wire. At times teams from town would go in to play the prisoners, but mostly teams of prisoners played each other. A few town folk would gather in their cars outside the fence and watch.

There were unknown mysteries about the prison that fascinated us kids. We loved to watch when someone was going into the prison. Whether it was visitors, prisoners coming in from fields around town where there were prison farms, or a new inmate, they all went in through the main gate. Right over the main entry gate was a tower with windows all around and at least one or two guards on duty. The tower guard would lower a huge key, which must have been six or seven inches long, down the outside wall.

Those with authority to enter would remove the key from the hook on the end of the chain, push it into the lock, turn it, and swing open the gate. Inside the tower was a vestibule where visitors or incoming inmates were locked in. The guard would lock the outside gate to the street. Then the guard in the tower would lower the chain with the hook inside the vestibule through a hole in the floor and draw the key back up into the tower. When the key to the exterior door was gone, a guard inside would open a second door, and those coming in could pass into the prison courtyard. When one left the prison, the process was reversed.

We were fascinated by the guards who walked confidently from one tower to another along the top of the wall. There were no handrails, and from our viewpoint it looked as though the walkway on top was about a foot wide, though it must have been much wider. If one had any fear of heights, it was a bad place to work.

Prisoners at the Montana State Penitentiary didn't wear stripes or even orange suits. They wore blue chambray shirts and jeans. The only distinctive they had on their clothing from hundreds of farmers around the valley was the white stripe down both legs of the pants. The men also wore heavy denim jackets and work boots.

"Trustees" were prisoners who had proved their willingness to cooperate with the program and to work. Some of them worked across the street at the Registrar of Motor Vehicles. They were file clerks and had other mysterious duties in the back of the huge room where vehicles were registered for the entire state. I worked there for a while right after high school. We had strict instructions not to talk with the prisoners about anything other than business. But there were always a couple of girls behind the file cabinets flirting with them.

There were several prison farms around the valley where trustees provided the labor. There was a pig farm just three miles north of town. I dated a young man whose father, a civilian, operated the farm. The family got to live in a house on the farm as part of the benefits package. For a while it made me nervous to go there, but after a while I realized that any prisoner who wanted to escape would not come to the house. Rather, the prisoner would likely take off and follow the river for a long time until he could find some clothing to change into and make a full escape.

There was also a cattle ranch out west of town where trustees raised enough beef to supply not only the prison but also the tuberculosis sanitarium and the state mental hospital located in the valley. I worked at the TB sanitarium for several summers during college, and part of the benefits there were marvelous meals that were free to employees. I have never eaten so much beef before or since that time. We could have all we wanted. The thinking was that employees needed to stay healthy so no TB bug could ever catch them.

There were also farm operations to provide feed for the cattle and gardens to provide all the fresh vegetables the prison needed. We grew quite used to seeing a field filled with trustees all hoeing away at rows and rows of cabbage or potatoes. Besides these enterprises, inmates made beautiful, hand-tooled leather goods, beaded work, and a number of other crafts. These were sold across the street at the prison office and provided a little income to the inmates for cigarettes and stamps for letters home.

The prison also had a band that practiced every Sunday afternoon. In the summer when the windows and doors of our house were open, we could hear the music wafting over the walls and across the river to our house. We got used to it and never thought what a privilege it was to have band music every Sunday afternoon. The prison band would have concerts periodically and, just once, I went. I was shocked to look up at the ceiling of the theatre and find a plaque that said, "Do Not Abandon Hope." For me that said it all.

* * *

Life went along with a great deal of normality in our sleepy little town. It felt pretty safe most of the time. But one afternoon during the summer of 1959, our quiet life exploded when the prisoners staged a major riot.

I had graduated from high school a couple of years before, and because I couldn't decide what I wanted to do with the rest of my life, I went to work—first at the registrar's office across the street from the prison, and then at the telephone company where I was a customer service rep. At that time we still had a manual switchboard, and my desk was close enough to the switchboard to hear the operators say, "Number please ... thank you." I can still hear the sound of those connecting cords sliding back into the console when a call ended and the operators disconnected the cords.

On the day of the riot, I left work at about five in the evening. Just a few minutes later, our switchboard exploded (so to speak). Somehow word got out that prisoners were holding guards as hostages and barricading themselves. The phone lines hummed with local calls as worried friends and relatives of the guards who worked in the prison called each other with news and fears. Soon it was the regional newspapers that called, and within hours it was the national and then international news agencies that were clogging the switchboard. I don't remember all the news agencies that showed up, but one of them was *Life* magazine.

The rioting went on for several days and seemed to get worse and worse. Deputy Warden Theodore Rothe was shot and killed, and Warden Powell was temporarily held hostage. We heard that prisoners had put mattresses over the windows of one of the towers in the cell block. They had taken guns from the guards and were fully armed. At one point we learned they had aimed their rifles at the 4-Bs Cafe that sat kitty-corner across the street from the prison. We figured out the time and were pretty sure that Glen had been sitting in that restaurant—a popular hangout for teens—at just that moment. They didn't fire into the restaurant, but it would have been an easy shot if they had decided to do so.

Finally, the National Guard was called in to quell the uprising. The Guard brought Bazooka guns with them, and sometime close to midnight when Deer Lodge was sleeping and the prisoners relaxed a little, the militia fired into the prison. Shells from the Bazookas hit the area of the cellblock where the prisoners were holed up. Then the soldiers stormed the prison and took control. One of the most exciting events ever to happen in my life in that little town came to an abrupt end.

The prison was in continuous use from the late 1800s to the early 1960s. In August 1959, the same year as the riot, the prison was severely damaged by a big earthquake (7.3 on the Richter Scale) that hit Yellowstone Park—the same one that created Quake Lake in a day when a mountain came down and formed a dam across a river. Shortly thereafter, the prison was deemed unsafe. Whether it actually was or not, the old structure was evacuated and the prison facility was moved to the countryside west of town. The Old Territorial Prison then became a museum, and it operates as such today.

26

Giants and Gemstones

Montana is a lot of things, and one of them seems to be a graveyard for paleontology treasures. More dinosaurs have been discovered in Montana than in any other state. There are ankylosaurs, T-Rex dinosaurs, mastodons, sabretooth tigers, and on and on. Use a computer search engine to take a look at "Montana Dinosaurs," and you will be amazed at the number of these earth giants that have been found in Montana.

Duck-Bill Dinosaurs

You can find duck-billed dinosaurs in Montana. For example, there's Leonardo, a mummified, seventy-seven-million-year-old duck-billed dinosaur who was only about three or four years old when he died. He was discovered July 27, 2000, during the Judith River, Montana, Dinosaur Institute Expedition.

Leonardo is a spectacular *brachylophosaurus* specimen. He is so perfectly preserved that you can see rare skin, scales, muscle, footpads—and even the contents of his stomach. It appears his last meal was of ferns, conifers, and magnolias. Also found inside his stomach was the pollen of forty plants. Of course, the actual tissue of Leonardo's body decayed over 11,000 years ago and was replaced by minerals. So what the scientists are studying is the fossil of a mummy—a condition that is rare in dinosaur finds.

Just because Leonardo was young when he died doesn't mean he was small. He weighed nearly two tons and was twenty-two feet long. The five-sided fossilized scales on his body range in size from the size of a BB to the size of a dime. And it appears he had a sail frill running up his back.

T-Rex

In 2002, a ranch owner discovered a mysterious bone that was later identified as the toe bone of a T-Rex. The rancher contacted a paleontologist who specialized in dinosaurs. Soon parts of the pelvis, both legs, and tail were also found. A number of T-Rex dinosaurs have been found in Montana—five at one location near Fort Peck Dam.

Mastodons

And then there are mastodons, which resemble elephants. They are about the same size as today's elephants and have trunks and tusks. They lived about 11,000 years ago. When I was in junior high, we learned that a local gravel pit three miles from home had uncovered ancient bones. The owner had the sense to call researchers from the University of Montana, who brought a team of paleontologists and students and began excavating the bones.

I had no idea what a mastodon was. When I learned, I was fascinated to discover that elephant-like creatures had roamed our little valley. I just couldn't imagine it—what with the cold winters and the distance from any vegetation even remotely tropical. But there was the evidence poking its way out of the ground. I was fascinated enough to go and watch the scientists at work with their small trowels, paintbrushes, and other soft brushes. They gently whisked away the soil, revealing inch by inch the jawbone and tusk of this creature who no doubt walked the very ground where our house stood.

At that time I developed a great love of paleontology, archeology, and scientific investigation of all things ancient. I have never been able to saturate this curiosity that was born in me at that time. Many years later when my children were young, we visited Dinosaur National Monument in Vernal, Utah. There, under a roof constructed over a dig site, I was stunned to learn that one man had spent thirty years working on a single skeleton. I'm not sure I could ever find enough dedication to spend thirty years on a five-foot square patch of ground.

The farther the scientists dig into that cliff in Utah, the more they discover. As recently as 2010, a team of paleontologists from Dinosaur National Monument, Brigham Young University, and the University of Michigan announced the discovery of a new, large plant-eating dinosaur called *Abydosaurus mcintoshi*.

But back to Montana. Montana is called the "Treasure State" with good reason. Treasures of all kinds are everywhere, and only some of them are ancient bones. We've already talked about the gold, silver, and other minerals found in Montana, but there are other treasures—gemstones—hidden in the state's soil.

Agates

Agates are found in abundance in the southern and eastern portions of the state. Once in a while Dad would stop along the highway where a mountainside had been bulldozed away to make way the road, leaving a cliff of gravel. Invariably, we would find small moss agates in that gravel bank.

The tremendous volcanic activities that produce the conditions necessary for the formation of agates span millions of years. Agates are formed when silica from volcanic ash, water from rainfall or ground sources, and manganese, iron, and other mineral oxides (which form the bands and "pictures" in the agates) run into cavities and pockets left by bubbling lava. Trapped in the cooling lava, these ingredients and shapes become Montana's moss agates.

Iron oxide provides the red color in the stones, and manganese oxide the black. High-powered microscopes show tracings of little canals that once admitted water containing one or more of these metals in solution. When the water dried out, the canals in the stones closed, creating the fernlike effects and "pictures" of trees, shrubs, and mountains.

While agates are not faceted, they are cut and polished. Their hardness requires a diamond-beaded blade. Agates are becoming scarce, but spring rains and run-off conditions still turn up new agates in gravel beds and hillsides, especially along the Yellowstone River. Montana's blue agates are stunningly beautiful and come in all shades of blue from light blue to dark sapphire blue. Blue agates are rarer in Montana than the moss agate, but some can be found throughout southwestern Montana.

Sapphires

Montana's sapphires come in a variety of colors from pinks to bright blue. They are cut like diamonds to make jewelry. Montana sapphires were set into the Royal Crown Jewels of England. Although miners threw sapphires away during the gold rush days, they are now the most valuable gemstones found in America.

Crystals

Rock hounds in Montana search mostly for sapphires and agates, but there are many other treasures in the earth. About seventy miles from Butte is a designated rock-hunting site where rock hounds uncover beautiful crystals, amethysts, and smoky quartz crystals. It is an amazing experience to dig in the soil and turn up perfectly faceted six-sided crystals. You always hope to find a big purple one, which means you have found an amethyst. Many of the amethysts and quartz crystals found in Montana are of gem quality.

Garnets are found in many areas of Montana. Their official name is *pyrope-almandine* crystal, and they range from bright reds to pink or orange-tinted reds. There are heavy deposits of them at Alder Gulch in southwestern Montana, where one of the largest placer gold strikes in history was made. Garnets are also found in the Greenhorn and Tobacco Root mountain ranges. These gemstones may also be turned up at sapphires sites, so hunting for sapphires has the bonus for rock hounds of pocketing a few garnets during their hunt.

Several areas of Montana have calcite crystals. There are caves in the Pryor Mountains at the Wyoming/Montana border lined with these beautiful crystals. They are found just thirty miles from Deer Lodge in the Drummond area. Yellow barite crystals are in the Indian Head Rock area just west of Basin. It is also possible to find rubies among the state's gemstones.

* * *

The secret to finding Montana's vast treasures—whether the treasure is gemstones in the earth or an activity like skiing, hunting, fishing, hiking, or riding horseback—is to get out there and do it. My mother's words come back to me now: "If you want to have fun, you have to get out there and put forth a little effort." So true, Mom, so true.

27

Rodeos and All Things Western

There is no doubt about it—we three kids grew up in the Wild West. Many of our schoolmates wore cowboy hats and walked with a bow-legged waddle. They were as at home on a horse as they were in a car. They didn't play at being cowboys; they worked at it alongside their dads, brothers, sisters, and even their mothers. When it was branding time, everybody worked to bring the herds with new calves from the grazing lands in the mountains to the main ranch. There they would receive the ranch's brand on their rump, assuring no one would steal them.

The air was filled with the dust and sweat of both men and horses, the white-hot heat of the branding iron, the acrid smell of burning flesh, and the bawling of both calves and their mothers. After lassoing the calves, throwing them to the ground, and hog-tying them, the ranchers would apply the branding iron. In a couple of minutes it was all over and the freed calves returned to their anxious mothers, unless they were also due for dehorning and castration. That was a different story, but it was over in a hurry as well. Cattlemen had to move many calves through the process in a day, and there was no time to dawdle.

The year was not complete without a rodeo or two in the county. Deer Lodge had a rather nice rodeo at the fairgrounds right on the main street. The venue was small, so you could really get up close and personal—too much so sometimes. Once in a while a cowboy would spin on his quarter horse as he chased an errant cow, and the horse's hooves would spew dirt and gravel into the seats of the weathered gray grandstand—and into your face.

Then there was the bull riding. Bulls were bred to be the meanest, toughest, side-winding animals possible. Rodeo riding was serious business and was taken seriously. Cowboys who were successful on the circuit could make big money, and for many riders it was the mainstay of their incomes.

The first time I ever saw bull riding, I couldn't believe my eyes. I could see something happening in the chutes across the arena, but I couldn't tell what. I saw a cowboy climb on what I presumed to be the bull. There seemed to be quite a bit of adjusting going on, and then the gate opened and an explosion of furious beef came shooting out. Those bulls twisted, turned, hunched up, and stretched out as they tried to rid themselves of the rider.

The rider, with one hand holding onto a cinch rope and the other in the air, hung on for dear life and a paycheck. It was only ten seconds, but even sitting in the stands it seemed like an eternity. For those riders who didn't get bucked off, there was the problem of getting off—safely. A rider on horseback would come up beside the bull, pick the rider off, and take him to safety as he hung on the side of the rescue horse.

For those who got thrown before the official end of the ride, there was danger afoot with that four-footed, horned bellowing angry bull. That's where the rodeo clowns came in. Those fearless men would attract the maddened bull with a red kerchief or a waving hat until the bull gave up trying to gore the cowboy. When the bull turned his attention to the clowns and gave pursuit, they would run for the fence. If the fence was too far away, they would dive into a tube made of several tires hooked together to form a cylinder. The clowns let those old bulls pummel the tires and try to gore them through the spaces. If the cowboy was uninjured, he scampered away while all this was going on. If he was hurt, the clowns kept it up until the cowboy could be rescued. Then the bull was driven out of the arena. By this time he was usually willing to go. He'd had enough.

Every rodeo also had bronco riding. It was just as dangerous as bull riding, because the horses were more agile in their twists and turns as they tried to dislodge the rider. They were less dangerous only because they had no horns. An angry bronc could still trample underfoot a fallen cowboy.

* * *

One rodeo was held in Helmville, Montana. Helmville is in the north end of Powell County, while Deer Lodge is in the south end. Every Labor Day, the farmers and cowboys of the north area would get together and practice their everyday skills in some of the funnest and funniest rodeo events ever. The little kids participated by sheep riding. For them, the challenge was every bit as great as riding an angry bull. Another event not found in every rodeo was trying to milk wild cows. The wild cows were not accustomed to having cowboys pull at their teats, trying to extract a measurable amount to put in their pop bottles. It was hilarious to watch tough, rugged Montana cowboys chasing cows and trying to get them to cooperate with the plan.

* * *

Growing up in Montana, I didn't give much thought to the unique lifestyle we lived. It was just the way things were. I thought everybody's friends rode in rodeos and wore cowboy boots, hats, and fitted shirts with snaps rather than buttons. Now that I've lived in multiple places across the continent, I realize what a wild, challenging life we lived.

The good news is that life hasn't changed much in Montana. Yes, the Internet and cell phones are there—though cell phone service may be a little spotty. Yes, you can find designer coffee if you look hard enough. Yes, you can see Hollywood movies—if you wait long enough. There are too many ATVs and snowmobiles running around the woods for some people's taste. But much of life remains the same as the fiercely independent people of Montana scratch their living out of the dust and rocks of the glacial land.

The cowboys still go out and saddle up each day to do their work. Rodeos only come once a year, but the ranch demands their attention every day—rain or shine, freezing cold or boiling heat. Animals have to be fed and cared for. Crops have to be put in. Hay has to be cut and stacked. Potatoes have to be picked. And so the people do it. Most of them love the life they have chosen and would never live any other way.

28

Swimming Holes

One of my favorite stories Dad used to tell was about going swimming when his mother had forbidden him from doing so. She had told Dad's brother (Wayne), sister (Juanita), and Dad—the "fearsome trio"— not to swim in the ponds they might find on their way home from school, no matter how hot it was or how inviting the water might look.

One day, the temptation to cool off in a convenient pond was just too much. They knew that if they went swimming in their clothes their mother would know they had disobeyed her, and it never occurred to them to go swimming in the nude. There was an old shed nearby the pond, so they went in to look for something to fashion into bathing suits. What they found were gunny sacks. They managed to cut or tear holes in them for their arms and head, and then they fastened everything together with nails.

The three ran for the pond and jumped in all together. Those heavy gunny sacks began to absorb water and get heavier and heavier. The situation became life threatening as the trio tried to get their heads above water. It is a wonder they didn't drown. Somehow they managed to get out of the pond, and their mom never learned what they had done. They were cured forever of swimming without permission, and it was then they gave up any hope of becoming swimsuit designers.

We used to find swimming holes here and there as well. Usually they were more like dip-your-toe-in ponds, as the water was always snow-fed and so cold. But there was one place we loved. It was about forty miles from home and right beside the highway near Drummond, Montana. Trucks roared up and down the highway right beside our swimming hole.

The place was called Bearmouth Hot Springs, though it really wasn't terribly hot. The water was about sixty-eight to seventy-five degrees—pleasant for swimming.

The pond was deep—about twenty feet deep—and the water was crystal clear. Towering red limestone rock walls flanked one side of the pond, and someone had put a kind of diving board at one end. Once, when I was sitting on the end of the diving board dragging my feet through the water, I discovered there was something else on the other end of the board—a muskrat. I screamed and scared the poor little thing into the bushes. That was the last I saw of him.

Another place we loved to swim was at Conley Lake. Conley Lake was a part of a 33,000-acre ranch that had once been owned and operated by the infamous Frank Conley, the warden of the Montana State Penitentiary in Deer Lodge from 1890 to 1921. The lake and his home were fascinating places. Mom told me about visiting the Conley estate at this little lake when she was a teenager and about a room with a long row of brass beds in it. So, of course, I had to go exploring. Sure enough, I found the room and the beds all in a row. Some kind of dormitory for guests, I suppose.

Ironically, the ranch, all its buildings, and the lake are now part of the Montana State Prison system. In 1973, after the big earthquake of 1959, funds were allocated to build a new prison on the ranch, and in 1974 construction began on a new facility three miles outside of town. It took five years to build the new prison. On September 5, 1979, the last inmates were moved from the old facility to the new one.

I'm not sure who owned the ranch at the time I was growing up. All I know is that once or twice I was able to join a group of other teens at the lake to picnic and swim there. There was a float raft not far off shore, and we would swim out there and sit on it.

Conley Lake fed a stream called Tin Cup Joe Creek, which fed a little pond we called "Smiling Pond." Well, to be truthful Smiling Pond was a pretty sad excuse for a pool or a pond. It was full of junk—old tires, wood, and pieces of iron. However, it was only a couple of blocks from the house, and my brothers would go there and build rafts from the flotsam found there. I don't think they ever swam in it, but you'd have to ask them.

Most of our swimming—and there was a lot of it—happened at the Deer Lodge public schools swimming pool. The pool had been a Works Progress Administration (WPA) project, and it was pretty special for a small town like ours to have it. It wasn't large, but we loved it. During the summer, continuous classes were held at the pool. After I learned to swim there, completed a water safety program, and began to compete in some of the swimming events around the state, I worked a couple of summers at the pool.

A workday at the pool went something like this. A big, heavy metal-clad door would open and a long line of little girls or boys—one or the other, and not both at the same time, as there was only one changing room—would open. Little bodies would line up at the window to get a towel and a blue cotton-knit tank-type swimming suits for the girls and shorts for the boys. We had them in three sizes: small, medium, and large. The kids would go back to the changing room to put on their suits, then they were sent through the showers, and finally they went through a footbath—a shallow indentation in the cement floor filled with some kind of potent disinfectant.

Those little bodies would line up and sit on a kind of tile bench that extended all around the pool and served as its edge. Finally, we would take the now-shivering little ones into the pool to give them their first swimming experiences. Oh, the joy in their eyes when they first floated all by themselves. Lessons, including suits and towels, cost something like three dollars for six weeks.

Older classes progressed through learning all the swimming strokes and diving. One of our teachers, Joanne Middleton, had a system of counting out the stroke movements. In my head, when I am thinking about the breaststroke, I hear her voice, "Pull, breathe, two, three, rest," for the arm movements. The leg movement was the frog kick, of course. On the "pull, breathe" part of the arm movements, we drew up our legs in a frog position; and then with the "two, three" count, we extended our legs and snapped them together. It worked, and I still find myself using the technique when teaching my grandchildren.

Later on we joined a swimming team and learned racing dives, flip turns, and back starts. Some swimmers could get a lot of bounce out of the low diving board on the pool. Some of the kids would jump as hard as they could on the end of the board and try to touch the rather low ceiling of the building. Personally, I never enjoyed diving, though I could do a fair front dive, a back dive, and a backflip.

Back to my workday. When the kids finished their lessons, they would go back through the shower and deposit their suits in a bucket. It was my job to collect the buckets of suits and wash and dry them in the machines that were situated at one end of the pool. Then I'd fold the suits and put them back on the shelf for the next day and the next round of kids. So, when I wasn't in the water with the kids, I was a washerwoman.

It all seems kind of primitive now, given the incredible modern facilities available to today's kids. However, in spite of the pool's limitations, we learned to swim. Ray learned to swim very well and even got a special dispensation to use the pool solo for training. As a safety factor, I remember sitting beside the pool when he was the only one in it, watching him go up and down the lanes as he built his endurance. Ray went to the University of Minnesota on a swimming scholarship, so that particular swimming spot—the Deer Lodge pool—was very good to him and to our family.

Some kids are given lots of things, and some kids have lots of great experiences. We were the latter kind, and while our possessions were always rather simple and often homemade, we were rich in experiences that have not worn out or been lost with time. It's a good formula for raising kids today.

29

A Forever Kind of Love

Mom never had another boyfriend, and Dad never had another girlfriend that he was serious about. They were married sixty-two years and could barely say goodbye to each other when the end came. It all began in Washington State near the Puyallup Bridge, and they never got over their love affair. It happened like this.

One of Mom's sisters had been ill with a nerve disease called "Saint Vitus Dance" (now Sydenham's chorea). It was helpful to her and the Cole family to get away from home for a while each summer. Grandfather Cole's railroad pass came in handy, and his family traveled to the west coast by train. Each summer, my grandmother would pack up all six kids and take them by train to Washington to pick berries. The family was given some kind of meager accommodations and meals, and they picked berries from sun-up until sundown.

There wasn't much to do in the berry fields of Washington, so the girls would go out for walks in the evening. One evening, Grace and Edith were walking along the road when an old car with two young guys stopped and asked them if they'd like a ride home. I can't imagine my mother saying yes quickly, but I can believe that her effervescent, daring sister, Edith, might have. Things were different in those days—the guys really just wanted to give the girls a lift and not take advantage of them. One of those young men, Orbrie, became my father, and the other, Orbrie's brother, Wayne, became my uncle. Eventually, when Wayne's five children were born and we three were as well, there were eight double-cousins all named Ellis.

I suppose the guys saw the girls during the next few weeks. We don't know, but after the family returned to Deer Lodge, Montana, it wasn't long until Wayne showed up and began seriously courting sixteen-year-old Edith. Grandma Cole wasn't very excited about that, but it happened anyway.

One night when Grace and Edith had gone up to bed, Edith turned and said to my mom, "Do you want to see something?" She showed her a wedding ring.

"Are you married, Edith?" Grace asked.

"Yes, I am."

Grace couldn't believe it. Here was her next-in-age sister getting married and then coming home to her own bed. Well, that wouldn't work, so Grace got out of bed and went to her mother. "Edith's married," she told her. Of course, no one in the family believed it, but Grandma Cole went to Edith.

"Are you married?" she asked. Edith affirmed that she was, so Grandma figured out how to help the newlyweds have a place of their own in her house.

About the same time, Orbrie moved to Montana. He had not forgotten the young girl he had met by the side of the road. She was only fourteen and he was seventeen when they began dating. They dated for six years. When the time came for Orbrie to make the decision to marry, he wanted to be sure that Grace was God's choice for him. By this time they had both had a spiritual rebirth and were active in the little church newly begun in Deer Lodge. One evening, he was praying on his knees at the altar of the church. He said to God, "If Grace is your choice for me, have her come and stand next to me right now." Grace came instantly, without a clue and for no apparent reason. He knew then that she was God's choice for him.

They began to plan their wedding. Somewhere my mother had gotten some ideas about style and the nice way to do things. It probably came from working for a banker's wife and helping her with table setups for guests and just talking about the finer things of life. At any rate, Grace wanted a white gown and a veil for her wedding. She also wanted a church wedding and a reception. And she had them. She was married in a white satin dress that must have been about a size six. It had mutton-chop sleeves, a standup collar, a high waist in the front, and princess lines. The veil was extremely simple—just white ribbons, tiny flowers, and tulle. Daddy wore a dark-colored suit. He was tall—six-foot-one—and very slender with a real wedge shape, broad shoulders, and not much bottom. They were a striking pair.

Their reception was held at Grandma Cole's house on Main Street, where long tables had been spread out between the kitchen and living room. Friends and family were there to wish the newlyweds well. They honeymooned in Washington State.

Daddy always had the utmost respect for Mother. He used to say, "I've heard men say awful things about their wives—calling them 'the old lady.' I didn't begin to live until I married Grace." It seemed they were happiest when they were out in the woods together doing something: cutting wood, hunting, fishing, picking berries, building their cabin. We kids were a wild bunch, running here and there and yelling through fields and woods. Sometimes we would look back to see them coming up the path holding hands.

Mother had strong ideas about what she wanted to do, and she could be a handful when she set her mind on something. Sometimes Daddy just gave in and let her have her way, but sometimes he would say, "Grace, Grace . . . you can't do that." And she wouldn't. Sometimes he could be morose, introspective, and almost sad. Sometimes he could be a rambunctious wild man, charging around and banging things or disappearing to the shop or the woods to cool off. But most of the time he provided the stability and security that was our family, and she provided the verve and fun along with superb care of us kids. And they loved each other.

They had their share of scary things happen. Ray stuck his hand in hot ashes when he was just a toddler. Glen was pinned under a grindstone that toppled over on him. He had mumps meningitis encephalitis and took a couple of years to recover. Dad had to have a ruptured disk removed and couldn't work for several months.

Somehow, on a meager income, they managed to put three kids through college and amass more money than they could use in a lifetime. They always paid their tithes to the church. They gardened, hunted, and fished to keep the costs of feeding a growing family low. Mom sewed and could make garments that were superbly tailored and would last longer than any I've ever known. Mom and Dad took Yankee thrift to a fine art.

When they grew older, they got to see many of their grandchildren married and establishing their homes. They lived to see a few of their great-grandchildren born. But old age wasn't particularly kind to them. Dad joked, "The Bible said two would be one. Now it takes the two of us to make one." His hearing failed; hers was acute. He couldn't walk well as the cartilage wore away in his knees; she was too spry, climbing on chairs and ladders and walking fast. Her mind began to fail; his was sharp to the last week of his life. She forgot almost everything; he remembered the smallest details.

They went to church together. They went to the senior citizens' center for lunch together. They had people in and went out to others' homes. They went snowmobiling and ice fishing long after the time most seniors are sitting in rocking chairs. They went to camp meetings and other church events. They encouraged, prayed for, and counseled others.

They won the respect of everyone who knew them, especially their family. When family members struggled with life, it was to Grandma and Grandpa they went, regardless of whether the struggle was awful or was a challenge in work or life. Quietly and wisely, they counseled the struggling souls and were always there for the people they loved.

Dad became ill with prostate cancer. He tried to care for Mom long after he should have stopped, but in some way she gave meaning to his struggle to live. When at last he could no longer do it and she had to go to a care facility, he lost his will to live. There just didn't seem to be any purpose in any of it.

Then he, too, went to the same care facility. Because he loved her so much, and she was so distressed to be away from him even for a few minutes, and it distressed him to see her distressed, they had to be kept apart most of the time. But when she saw him, she kissed him and loved him. She was confused about a lot of things, but never about her love for him, nor he about his love for her. None of us will ever forget the night when his life hung so low. She came to him and sang Brahms' lullaby. Then she said, "Orb, God has always taken care of us, and he always will."

Finally, when he laid down his life, we took her to see him one last time. She seemed to understand. She touched his forehead and said, "He's still warm." She kissed him goodbye, and we took her out. In her dementia, she never stopped looking for him—the love of her life—until the moment she too slipped away. What a reunion those two must have had within the gates of heaven. Their tombstone says it all. It reads, "Together forever with the Lord they loved."

EPILOGUE

All Things Come to an End

It was a lovely springtime-in-the-Rockies kind of day when my brothers and I met in Montana to close down the home place. Sixty years before this time, Mom and Dad had plunked down their down payment on the small two-bedroom brown-and-white bungalow on a half-acre of ground that we still call "home."

I was only a little more than three years old when we moved in, but I remember the excitement of that real bathroom. I thought a bathtub was about the greatest thing I had ever seen. A real bathtub in a real bathroom with a closing door and a flushing toilet!

Over the years, the house was modernized, expanded, and painted until it looked more like a 1950s ranch than it did a bungalow. Dad added other buildings to the property. A two-car garage with a garage door opener took the place of the tiny one that had been through a fire and had cardboard nailed over the charred wood. When Dad built the garage, he put in an attic. Then he and Mom began to fill it with things that should have been thrown out or given away.

Packrats will gather up bits and pieces of shiny foil, strings, or other things and take them to their nests. Some people are packrats, and some people are super-packrats. Daddy was a super-packrat. He stored pieces of wire, baling twine, nails, screening materials, handles from discarded brooms, and worn out tools until his workshop was stuffed full of stuff. Outside and back of this workshop, there was a small service yard that held old washtubs, a wagon wheel or two, old stoves, and stove parts. Don't get the idea it looked like a junkyard. It didn't. Everything was neatly stored and screened from public view.

Dad had added one more building on the property: a woodshed where he stored the cords and cords of wood used to fire the woodstove he and Mother used the last twenty years they lived in the house. He had cut every piece of this wood by hand, loaded it on his pickup truck, and brought it from the mountains into town, where it was neatly stacked in this covered open-sided building.

My brothers and I were with Dad for the last ten days as his life ebbed away. When the funeral was over, we knew we needed to get back to our jobs. We decided to close up the buildings and come back in the spring when new life was pushing up from the ground. We'd deal with the disposal of their property when our emotions were not quite so raw and our grief not so deep.

So here we were this bright sunny day in May, looking at the garage floor where the flotsam of the past sixty years had been piled up more than a year before. Now we had to deal with it. The only problem was that the stuff had been sitting on the garage floor all through the long winter, and now mice had invaded it. There was evidence of mouse occupation everywhere. They had even crawled up through the floorboards of the pickup and left their calling cards inside.

In addition to boxes of raw wool used for quilt-making, clothing that should have been thrown out ages ago, and a lot of other nest-building materials, there was also a fifty-five gallon drum half full of grain. When Daddy would find a bag of grain that had fallen off some farmer's truck and burst open, he'd stop, shovel it up, and bring it home. Then, when he was on the way to his cabin, he'd grab a bucket of grain and take it to spread for the wild turkeys that hung out there. For some reason, he had not put a lid on the top of the barrel, but he had thrown in orange-colored baling twine. Mice had crawled down in that twine and made some pretty elaborate nests of string, wool, paper, plastic, and snippets of clothing. In that barrel was all the grain many generations of mice could ever eat. The whole place was mouse heaven for sure.

My sister-in-law, Dorothy, and I were sorting through boxes when she screamed. As she bent over a box, a mouse had scampered out and headed for the door. I was between the mouse and the door. "Look out, he's coming your way!" she yelled. I stepped back, right into his path. He didn't run up my pants leg, but I thought he would. After another mouse jumped out of the box and fled, my brother Glen took a pitchfork and used it to fish the nests out of the barrel. The second time he stuck the pitchfork down in the barrel, another mouse shot out. About that time Ray showed up. He got right into the hunt when another mouse jumped out of the barrel and ran into a pile of shingles. We had no idea how many more mice escaped, but soon things quieted down and all that was left was "evidence" that the mice had been there.

Five days later, after we had laughed over some of Dad's "inventions," cried over our parents' worn-out clothing, and hauled truckloads of stuff to the dump and Goodwill in a neighboring town, we made our selections from the things that were left.

Ray chose the old wood stove that had once stood in the living room—the same stove where we had heated our clothing on cold winter mornings before putting them on. Ray also wanted Mom and Dad's car and some tools.

I chose the eleven-pound featherweight Singer sewing machine that Mom had used to sew upholstery, leather, and who knows what else. This was the machine I had used when I learned to sew, and it still works like a dream. I took Dad's chair, the table we ate on when I was a child (which had been remodeled into a sofa table), and the highchair my grandfather had found for me when I was a baby.

There were no treasures here. What we took away were the nostalgic remembrances that bound us to this place. Our task was made somewhat easier, as Glen had decided to keep the home place as a retreat for his family. So we knew that when we could visit, a lot of Mom's and Dad's familiar things would be there waiting us.

Then it was done. There was no more to clean up. We stood in the yard to say goodbye, and then Ray and I climbed into the rental truck to drive to Minneapolis. Dorothy looked at me with tears pouring down her face and said, "It's over, isn't it? It's truly over." I could only whisper around the lump in my throat, "Yes, it's over." In my mind, I could hear some of my father's last words to me as the entire family had sat beside a fire, roasting ears of corn from his garden. He had said, "You work your whole life to get all this stuff, and then in the end you have to just walk away from it."

Ray and I climbed into our rented truck, and pulling a trailer with the folks' Ford sedan on it, we drove off with our strange treasures. Somewhere out across the barren prairies of eastern Montana, it began to sink in that "life does not consist of an abundance of things." It wasn't the stuff Mom and Dad left behind that was important, it was the love. What we treasured most were the values they had given us: their work ethic, their passion for life and adventure, their compassion and strong desire to help the unfortunate. We had inherited a treasure trove of intangible qualities. The stuff we took away will eventually vanish into dust, but what those two stalwart Montanans put in us will last forever.

— The End —

Fifty Bests About Montana

1. Montana has the largest migratory elk herd in the nation.

2. The state boasts the largest breeding population of trumpeter swans in the lower United States.

3. At the Rocky Mountain Front Eagle Migration Area west of Great Falls, more golden eagles have been seen in a single day than anywhere else in the country.

4. North of Missoula is the largest population of nesting common loons in the western United States.

5. The average square mile of land in Montana contains 1.4 elk, 1.4 pronghorn antelope, and 3.3 deer.

6. The Freezeout Lake Wildlife Management Area contains as many as 300,000 snow geese and 10,000 tundra swans during migration.

7. At Bowdoin National Wildlife Refuge, it is possible to see up to 1,700 nesting pelicans.

8. The Montana Yogo Sapphire is the only North American gem to be included in the Crown Jewels of England.

9. In 1888, Helena had more millionaires per capita than any other city in the world.

10. Forty-six out of Montana's fifty-six counties are considered "frontier counties," with an average population of six or fewer people per square mile.

11. Dinosaur eggs have been discovered at Egg Mountain near Choteau, supporting the theory that some dinosaurs were more like mammals and birds than like reptiles.

12. Montana is the only state with a triple divide, allowing water to flow into the Pacific Ocean, Atlantic Ocean, and Hudson Bay. This phenomenon occurs at Triple Divide Peak in Glacier National Park.

13. Henry Plummer, the notorious outlaw, built the first jail constructed in the state.

14. No state has as many different species of mammals as Montana.

15. The moose, now numbering more than 8,000 in Montana, was thought to be extinct in the Rockies south of Canada during the 1900s.

16. Flathead Lake in northwest Montana contains more than 200 square miles of water and 185 miles of shoreline. It is considered the largest natural freshwater lake in the west.

17. Miles City is known as the cowboy capitol.

18. Yellowstone National Park in southern Montana and northern Wyoming was the first national park in the nation.

19. The town of Ekalaka was named for the daughter of the famous Sioux chief Sitting Bull.

20. Fife was named after the type of wheat grown in the area or, as some locals contend, by Tommy Simpson for his home in Scotland.

21. Fishtail was either named for a Mr. Fishtail who lived in the area or, as the area Indians prefer, for some of the peaks in the nearby Beartooth Mountain Range that look like the tail of a fish.

22. The Yaak community is the most northwestern settlement in the state.

23. Montana has the largest grizzly bear population in the lower forty-eight states.

24. Near the Pines Recreation Area, as many as 100 sage grouse perform their extraordinary spring mating rituals.

25. The first luge run in North America was built at Lolo Hot Springs on Lolo Pass in 1965.

26. Combination, Comet, Keystone, Black Pine, and Pony are names of Montana ghost towns. Two Dot and Lame Deer are not ghost towns . . . yet.

27. Virginia City was founded in 1863 and is considered to be the most complete original town of its kind in the United States.

28. Montana is nicknamed the "Treasure State."

29. The bitterroot is the official state flower.

30. The density of the state is six people per square mile.

31. The highest point in the state is Granite Peak at 12,799 feet.

32. The most visited place in Montana is Glacier National Park, known as the crown jewel of the continent. It lies along Montana's northern border and adjoins Waterton Lakes National Park in Canada, forming the world's first International Peace Park.

33. Buffalo in the wild can still be viewed at the National Bison Range in Moiese, south of Flathead Lake and west of the Mission Mountains.

34. Montana's first territorial capital, Bannack, has been preserved as a ghost town state park along once gold-laden Grasshopper Creek.

35. The Old West comes to life through the brush and sculpture of famed western artist Charlie Russell at the Charles M. Russell museum complex in Great Falls. The museum contains the world's largest collection of Russell's work, his original log-cabin studio, and his Great Falls home.

36. The Museum of the Rockies in Bozeman gained fame through the work of its chief paleontologist, Jack Horner. Horner was the prototype for the character Dr. Alan Grant in the best selling novel/movie *Jurassic Park*.

37. Montana's rivers and streams provide water for three oceans and three of the North American continent's major river basins.

38. Just south of the city of Billings, Lt. Col. George Armstrong Custer and his troops made their last stand. Little Bighorn Battlefield National Monument features the Plains Indians and United States military involved in the historic battle.

39. The western meadowlark is the official state bird.

40. The first inhabitants of Montana were the Plains Indians.

41. Montana is home to seven Indian reservations.

42. Every spring, nearly 10,000 white pelicans with a wingspan of nine feet migrate from the Gulf of Mexico to Medicine Lake in northeastern Montana.

43. The Going to the Sun Road in Glacier Park is considered one of the most scenic drives in America.

44. The state's official animal is the grizzly bear.

45. The state's motto "Oro y Plata" means gold and silver.

46. Montana's name comes from the Spanish word for "mountain."

47. In Montana the elk, deer, and antelope populations outnumber the humans.

48. Glacier National Park in Montana has 250 lakes within its boundaries.

49. Hill County has the largest county park in the United States. Beaver Creek Park measures ten miles long and one mile wide.

50. Competing with the D River in Lincoln City, Oregon, for the title of the world's shortest river, the Roe River flows near Great Falls. Both rivers' lengths vary from fifty-eight feet to 200 feet. The source for this small river is Giant Springs, the largest freshwater spring in the United States.

Adapted from 50states.com http://www.50states.com/facts/mont.htm

To Order More Copies

If you liked *Montana's Child: A Memoir of Life in Big Sky Country* and want to share the story with friends and family, you can order it through amazon.com. A Kindle edition is also available.

OTHER BOOKS BY THE AUTHOR

Simply Fun for Families, Revell
The Christmas Flower, Strang Communications
La Flor De Pascua (Spanish) Strang Communications.
Read and Share Bible, Tommy Nelson
Read and Share Toddler's Bible, Tommy Nelson
Read and Share Devotional, Tommy Nelson
Christmas Angels, Tommy Nelson
Streams in the Desert, Zonderkidz
Bible Adventures, Reader's Digest
Our Daily Bread, Reader's Digest
Noah's Animal Friends, Reader's Digest
The First Christmas, Reader's Digest
I Can Learn Bible Stories, Reader's Digest
Jesus Is Alive, with Josh and Sean McDowell, Regal Books
Growing in the Fruit of the Spirit (Bible Study),
Gospel Light for First Place 4 Health

Ghost written:
Bod for God, Gospel Light
Get off the Couch, Gospel Light
A Little Child Shall Lead Them, custom published for
Dr. Elizabeth Hynd of New Hope Centre, Swaziland.
24 Extraordinary Children, custom published for Dr.
Elizabeth Hynd of New Hope Centre, Swaziland.
Footprints on African Hearts and Soil, custom published
biography of Dr. Samuel Hynd, veteran missionary doctor
and founder of Acts II Aids Clinic, Swaziland: 2014.

If You Have a Story to Tell

At Seaside Creative Services, Inc. we offer multiple services to take your book from idea or manuscript all the way to print. We can also publish your book as a Kindle edition.. Contact us now we'll get started! If you don't need publishing services but still need editing help, we can work with you on any level. Please see our services below and contact us at seasidecreativeservices@gmail.com for more information.

Kindle E-books—We use any document or digital file that you have to format and upload your book to Amazon as a Kindle e-book.

Book Idea Development—Many people have an idea for a book, but they have absolutely no idea where to begin. That is where our team can help. Getting the basic idea/concept is probably the most important part of writing a book. We will help you develop a purpose for your book and will work with you to craft an outline that will bring your idea to life.

Book Coaching—Perhaps you have an idea and a rough outline and have started to write your book, but you are stuck. You don't know what to do next. You feel so alone. You don't know where to turn for help to get going again. You have come to the right place. Our team has spent nearly 40 years helping writers tell their stories. We will encourage you, give suggestions, and coach you through the tough passages and transitions to bring your book to life.

Ghost Writing—Maybe you have a story, but the idea of writing a book has no appeal to you. What you need is a ghost writer. Our writers have amazing skills at taking a pile of nothing but bits and pieces and crafting them into a book. Of course, a large part of this process will be interviewing the author to pull the story out of his or her mind and onto paper. There are many wonderful stories just waiting to be told. Hire one of our ghost writers to help you tell yours.

In-Depth Edits—If you have a rough draft of a book, but you know it needs some serious work—and most do—you need an editor who will edit the book in-depth. That means sentence structure, accuracy of information, spelling, grammar, and moving pieces around to get the story to flow better and avoid a "meanwhile back at the ranch" kind of writing that confuses the reader. An in-depth edit is all about making your book the most reader-friendly it can be.

Lighter Edits—are called copyedits. Every book needs a copyedit whether you are a professor of English at an Ivy League school or a first time author. We all have blind spots in style, spelling, and grammar. An extra pair of eyes is the best thing to assure your book will not have glaring errors that cause the reader to question how much attention you have paid to your work. Copyeditors also fact check to make sure you have made no mistakes.

Proofreading—Proofreading is a skill that not every editor has. Great proofreaders are those nit-picky, detailed individuals who just seems to know how to find every little mistake. There is nothing worse than getting a book in print and finding a mistake the first time you open a page. Everyone needs a good proofreader to go over his or her book.

Typesetting—Even if you are a great writer, editor, and proofreader, you will still need to have your book typeset. We can help you with that function. Typesetting includes choosing an interior design for your book, formatting such things as page numbers, headers, footnotes and endnotes, charts, photos, etc. Let us help you with this technical part of producing a book.

Cover Design—While we are not cover designers, we have connections with some superb designers and we will manage the cover design process for you. Cover design will include the opportunity to choose from several mock-ups.

Back Cover and Marketing Copy—We can write the information that goes on the back cover of your book. This information will be written to grab your reader's attention. We can also write your author bio as well as sell copy. The cover, both front and back, is your key marketing tool and these days must be designed to show up well on Internet sites. In addition you will probably want some well-written sell copy to put with the cover photo. Let us help you achieve the best cover and marketing copy possible to draw sales to your book.

Critiquing—Maybe you have an idea, but you don't know if it is worth the time you would have to spend to develop it into a book. Or maybe you already have something written but aren't sure you should go on. Our staff will carefully read through your manuscript offering suggestions for improving it and making it something you can be proud of.

Indexing (creating and numbering)—This is a rare skill to find, but absolutely essential to those technical books where readers need access to a lot of information quickly. An index is what you need. We have the skills to create and number an index for your book.

Scanning—Many people are into self-publishing these days. Some have books they have written earlier that they'd now like to see back in print. But what can be done? Re-keyboarding the entire book seems like an overwhelming task. What you need is someone to scan your book and then check to see that what was scanned is correct. This is the first step to self-publishing an already published book or uploading any book as a Kindle e-book.

Rewrites—Sometimes an author has the idea or the kernel of an idea, but the manuscript hasn't turned out as hoped. Perhaps what you need is a rewrite. A rewrite would include the editor working with you to identify problem areas and to find a solution for presenting the material in the best possible way.

Compiling—Gift books, memory books, compilations of poems, sermons, lectures. We can help you compile these, and help you find quotes, lyrics, poems, etc. to fill out the book. All team members have experience with developing gift books.

Study Guides—Even the best study material is wasted if the format is not conducive to easy access by the reader. Our entire team has worked at writing and formatting study materials. We know how it should be done and we can help you with your curriculum.

Gwen Ellis Is Available for Speaking

Because of Gwen's extensive background in publishing, she is often asked to in teach Creative Writing. She would love to speak and encourage your group on practical living, facing crisis times in your life, or in the area of writing and creativity.

Parenting for Family Fun
Great talk for young mothers!

Simply Fun for Families. Having fun with your kids is essential for passing your values to them and for establishing the kind of parent/child relationships that will last for a lifetime. Gwen shares ideas not only for having fun, but for saving time and money to make family fun more affordable and enjoyable.

Decorating on a Shoestring
For those who want to have a beautiful home without breaking the bank.

You can have a beautiful and more importantly comfortable home tailored to your family's style and it doesn't have to break the bank. There has been an explosion of decorating TV shows and books since Gwen first co-wrote the book, *Decorating on a Shoestring*. But, let's face it, many of the decorating schemes shown on TV wouldn't be practical nor would they fit your family's life style. Even after watching a show, you probably still don't know how to put it together. We'll give you some practical pointers for making your home décor your very own.

What to Do When the Doctor Says It's Cancer
For those who've have cancer, those who are in remission, and those who love people with cancer.

No question about it, cancer is scary business. But a great attitude is one of the best "medicines" to beat cancer. Learn how to care for your soul when going through cancer. Learn how to help and encourage those you love who are sick. Gwen tells her story and miraculous recovery.

Dress Like a Million Bucks Without Spending It
For anyone who's ever said, "I have nothing to wear."

Gwen wants to teach you how to shop in your own closet and find new outfits. She has lots of secrets about sources for finding great bargains. Let her encourage you to try your hand at updating your clothing using accessories and simple sewing techniques. She'll show you some of the fabulous finds that are in her closet and tell you how little she spent to get them.

Becoming A Woman of Influence
Who Are They and How Do I Get to Be One?

Today and all the way back through the pages of history to the very beginning, we find the remarkable stories of women of influence. How are these amazing individuals made? What causes them to rise to the crises presented them in their lives? How do they not only overcome, but excel in their endeavors? We desperately need women who are not afraid to stand up for moral principles, who boldly speak the truth, who change the way the world works and the way ordinary people live their lives. You too can become a woman of influence.

Writing Talks
For Anyone Who Wants to Be a Writer or Improve Writing Skills.

Gwen has spoken at writers' conferences for many years. She can talk about almost any kind of writing because she has experience in most areas of writing and publishing. Eight-hour sessions on Writing for Children and on Writing Non-Fiction have been very popular. She can also teach article writing, writing study guides, inspirational writing for gift books and greeting cards. She uses exercises to stimulate creativity, generate ideas, and help you analyze the market and target your writing for a particular market.

www.ingramcontent.com/pod-product-compliance
Lightning Source LLC
Chambersburg PA
CBHW050536300426
44113CB00012B/2135